MILLION DOLLAR

AUTHOR MARTIN DERRICK

MILLION-DOLLAR CLASSICS

THE WORLD'S MOST EXPENSIVE CARS

PHOTOGRAPHY SIMON CLAY

CHARTWELL
BOOKS

This edition published in 2013 by
CHARTWELL BOOKS
an imprint of BOOK SALES
a division of Quarto Publishing Group USA Inc.
276 Fifth Avenue Suite 206
New York, New York 10001
USA

Produced by BlueRed Press Ltd
Copyright © 2011 BlueRed Press Ltd
Author Martin Derrick
Photography Simon Clay and Tom Wood
Design by Diverse Design & Communications

ISBN-13: 978-0-7858-3051-1

10 9 8 7 6 5 4 3

Printed in Shenzhen, China.

Reprinted 2014 twice.

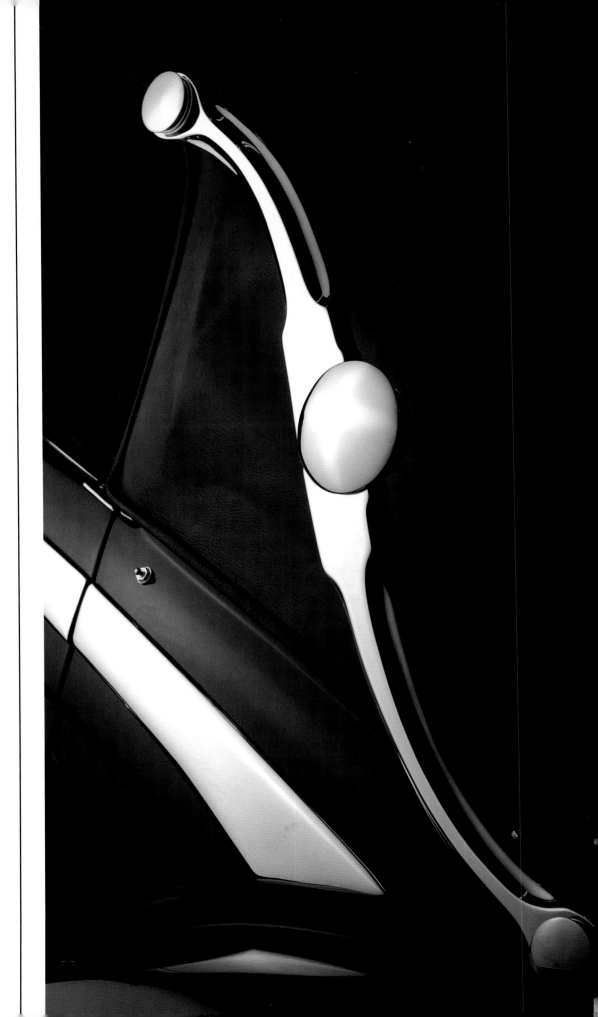

CONTENTS

1884 DE DION BOUTON ET TREPARDOUX DOS À DOS

Any car built in the nineteenth century is important historically but the prototype built in 1884 by De Dion, Bouton and Trepardoux at their factory at Puteaux to the west of Paris, is more significant than most. This is because the steam-driven machine not only heralded the start of one of the most significant companies in the early history of the automobile, but it is also reported to have won the world's very first motor race in 1887 when it covered the 19 miles (30km) course at an average speed of 26mph (42km/h).

There was, effectively, no bodywork. The car was built along the lines of a traditional carriage with a large water tank and a coke-fired vertical boiler at the front, and with two steam engines under the floor – each of the two engines, which worked in tandem, powered one rear wheel. The boiler was fuelled by coke, coal or wood and took some 40 minutes to raise enough pressure of steam to propel the car.

It seated four, with two passengers sitting behind the front seats and facing backwards, hence the car's name Dos à Dos, or "back-to-back" in French.

The Marquis Albert De Dion himself called the car "La Marquise", in honour not of his wife but of his mother, and he obviously held the vehicle in some affection because he kept it for many years, despite building many other cars in the decades that followed.

Trepardoux, the steam expert, left the company in 1894 when De Dion and Bouton made it clear they saw that the four-stroke internal combustion engine was the future of the automobile. They were right, and in due course De Dion-Bouton became the world's largest motor manufacturer, producing some 400 cars and 3,200 engines a year by 1900, and supplying engine technology to many other manufacturers.

La Marquise was recognised as a pioneering car early on, as it was proudly displayed at the Grand Exhibition held in Grenoble in 1925. It was later restored and brought to the UK where it won the UK National Steam Heritage Premier Award for Restoration and Preservation in 1991. Later still it claimed the honours at the 1997 Pebble Beach Concours' d'Elegance and was named by The Automobile Quarterly publication the "Most Historically Important Car at the Show".

It gained yet further honours at the 1996 Louis Vuitton Concours in London and since then it has regularly taken part in the annual London to Brighton Veteran Car Run where it was the oldest car to complete the course.

It was put up for sale at the 2007 Pebble Beach auction where it was sold for $3,520,000.

THE VETERAN CAR CLUB
OF GREAT BRITAIN

1884
DE DION BOUTON
& TRÉPARDOUX

CERT No. 1750

Country of Origin:	France
Body Design:	Traditional
Manufacture Date:	1884
Power:	2bhp (1.472kW) @ 5200rpm
Maximum Torque:	n.a.
Top Speed:	38mph (61km/h)
0-60mph (0-97km/h):	n.a.
Transmission:	Direct
Engine:	Two tandem steam engines
Length:	n.a.
Width:	n.a.
Wheelbase:	n.a.
Kerb Weight:	n.a.
Brakes:	None
Suspension:	Rigid axle (F); Rigid Axle (R)
Auction Sale:	2007 £2,288,000 (€2,682,592.00; $3,520,000)

1912 BUGATTI 5 LITRE

When Ettore Bugatti resigned from the Deutz company in Cologne in 1910 to set up his own works in Molsheim, he made clear in an open letter to his potential customers that he intended to build a completely new type of vehicle.

"Considering the enormous expense given rise to, until now, by fast and powerful cars", he wrote, "I have decided to create a new breed of light car, able to render the same services, enjoying the same qualities, the same freedom, but freed forever from that great source of expense: weight."

Sure enough, Bugatti's early Type 10 cars weighed in at just 349kg (769 lbs.) and were joined on the fledgling production line by revised and improved models including the Type 13 and Type 15 (one example of which, originally sold to Prince Hohenloe of Austria-Hungary in 1910 is today the world's oldest surviving Bugatti).

That year also marked what was probably the first competition entry of a Bugatti when M. Darritchon competed in the Gaillon Hill Climb in Normandy in a standard Type 13, when he came second in the touring car class. Soon Bugattis were appearing at other hill climbs and even in the French Grand Prix of 1911, where Ernest Friderich won his class.

Spurred by these early successes, Bugatti developed a car specifically for racing. Four examples of this Type 18 were completed between 1912 and 1914, fitted with a larger 5-litre engine with three valves per cylinder. Unusually these cars were chain-driven, the only Bugatti-badged cars to feature this drive method though the Type 8 Deutz that Ettore had designed was also chain-driven. The multi-plate clutch was also very similar to a design Bugatti had created for Deutz, though a different rear suspension set-up was chosen, with Deutz's semi-elliptic springs being discarded in favour of reversed quarter elliptic springs.

The first of these four competition cars was driven by Bugatti himself at the 1912 Mont Ventoux Hill Climb bear Avignon. The basic two-seater body was fitted with an elongated, tapering tail that may have helped in terms of aerodynamics but which provided no luggage space so when Bugatti drove the car from Molsheim to the event, he had to strap a leather case to the front of the car.

Bugatti was fourth fastest at Mont Ventoux, winning his class in a time of 19 minutes, 16.4 seconds for the 13.25 mile (21.3km) ascent.

Only a handful of Type 18 cars were built. This example, as driven by Bugatti himself, was estimated at between €1,800,000 and €2,400,000 when it came up for auction in 2009 but remained unsold.

Country of Origin:	France
Body Design:	Bugatti
Manufacture Date:	1912-14
Power:	100bhp (74.5kW) @ 2800rpm
Maximum Torque:	n.a.
Top Speed:	99mph (160km/h)
0-60mph (0-97km/h):	n.a.
Transmission:	4-speed manual
Engine:	5,027cc straight four
Length:	n.a.
Width:	n.a.
Wheelbase:	2550mm (100.4 in.)
Kerb Weight:	1250kg (2750 lbs.)
Brakes:	Rear drums
Suspension:	Live axe, semi-elliptical leaf springs and friction dampers (F); Live axle with reversed quarter-elliptic leaf springs (R)
Estimated Value:	£1.54–2.05 million (€1,8–2.4 million; $2.36–3.15 million)

1913 BUGATTI BLACK BESS
5 LITRE TYPE 18

In 1912 Ettore Bugatti, who had recently set up a factory at Molsheim in Alsace, started to build a small number of four-cylinder 5-litre cars, intended for competition use. He himself drove one to a class win at Mont Ventoux in 1912 and others were entered into the 1914 Indianapolis 500 and the 1915 Vanderbilt Cup and Grand Prix of California, though with little success.

The car was built along the lines of an earlier Deutz design (where Bugatti had been working before setting up on his own) and incorporated chain drive to the rear wheels — the only Bugatti to feature such an arrangement. The 5-litre four-cylinder engine with three valves per cylinder operated by an overhead camshaft produced 100bhp at 2,800rpm. This three-valve cylinder head design became almost a Bugatti trademark and was used in many of his most famous car, including the legendary Type 35.

Even as far back as 1912, Bugatti cars were renowned for their performance and it is believed that the maximum speed of the Type 18 may have been close to 100mph (161kmph) despite the fact that the cars were fitted with brakes to the rear wheels only.

But it wasn't so much outright performance that brought this car to the world's attention as the early owners of one particular example, which was originally delivered to French aviator Roland Garros in September 1913. He commissioned a compact torpedo body from the coachbuilding firm Labourdette but enjoyed little use of it as WWI broke out in 1914 and he was sadly killed just before the Armistice. The car was then sold to the chief engineer of the Sunbeam car company, Louis Coatalen and he in turn sold it to Ivy Cummings in 1919 who raced it in Britain until 1924 under the nick-name of "Black Bess".

It was then bought by LH Preston who raced it at Brooklands before selling it to the well-known actor James Robertson Justice. Later it was bought by the UK Bugatti Owners' Club President Colonel GM Giles who restored it before selling it for a meagre £200 to Rodney Clarke in 1938. Ten years later he sold it for £400 to Peter Hampton who maintained ownership until 1988 when it was sold to an unnamed Bugatti enthusiast.

Even without such an illustrious history, the 5-litre Bugatti would be a highly desirable car as only seven examples were built and only three are known to have survived to this day. Small wonder then, that it made $2,427,500 at the 2009 Bonhams sale at the Paris Retromobile show.

Country of Origin:	France	Width:	n.a.
Body Design:	Labourdette	Wheelbase:	2550mm (100.4 in.)
Manufacture Date:	1912-14	Kerb Weight:	1250kg (2750 lbs.)
Power:	100bhp (74.5kW) @ 2800rpm	Brakes:	Rear drums
Maximum Torque:	n.a.	Suspension:	Live axe, semi-elliptical leaf springs and friction dampers (F); Live axle with reversed quarter-elliptic leaf springs (R)
Top Speed:	99mph (160km/h)		
0-60mph (0-97km/h):	n.a.		
Transmission:	4-speed manual		
Engine:	5,027cc straight four	Auction Sale:	2009 £1,563,728 (€1,824,024; $2,427,500)
Length:	n.a.		

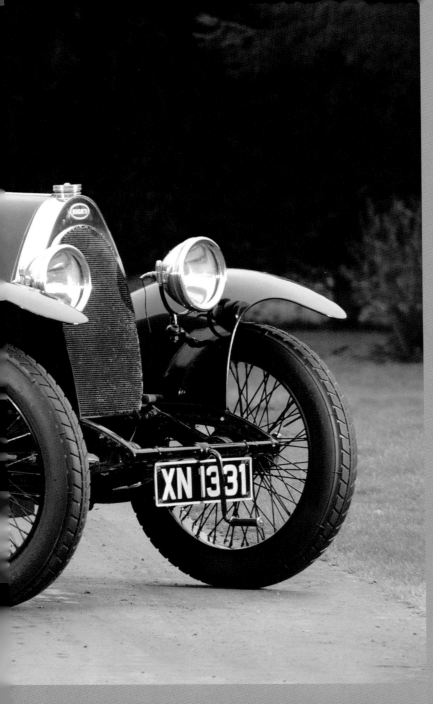

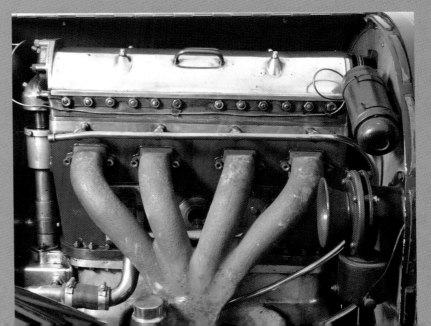

1930 DUESENBERG MODEL J DUAL COWL PHAETON

When Errett Lobban Cord bought the Duesenberg company in 1926 he had already restored and revitalised Auburn and he aimed to bring that same energy and single-minded commitment to dragging Duesenberg out of the post WWI economic doldrums.

The task he set the Duesenberg brothers was simple if highly ambitious: Build the world's finest automobile, better than Hispano-Suiza, Rolls-Royce or Bugatti. The brothers responded enthusiastically and created a car that not only lived up to Cord's expectations: It exceeded them. The Duesenberg Model J combined stunning performance (a top speed of well over 109mph or 175km/h) with the very finest engineering standards, beautiful coachbuilt bodies and the most luxurious of interiors.

Power came from a 6,882cc straight eight engine with twin overhead camshafts and four valves per cylinder that produced 265bhp, an enormous figure in those days. Customers ordered a chassis from the factory which cost $8,500 in 1929 when deliveries started and increased to $9,500 in 1931 – and this at a time when a basic Ford family saloon cost around $600! Once the chassis had been bought (every one of them was tested for 100 miles (161km) before it moved to the coachbuilders) customers then chose a body which cost anything from $3,000 to $20,000 on top of the chassis price.

One of those coachmakers was LeBaron which offered a number of different body styles for the Duesenberg J. They were built on either long or short wheelbase chassis and could be open or closed construction. Phaeton was the name given to four-seat convertibles, among the most popular of Duesenberg styles. Less common was the "barrel-side" body, on which the upper edge of the body is rolled towards the interior. It also features an unusual parallelogram moulding on the beltline. Only five such "Barrel-sides" were ever built, which makes this model J even more special.

The Duesenberg Model J was the ultimate in luxury, opulence and style and, needless to say, the province only of the wealthiest of the privileged elite. Even the contemporary advertising reflected this, with its single line of copy: "He Drives a Duesenberg" or "She Drives a Duesenberg".

The rarity and unique nature of Duesenbergs has been reflected in massively inflated values over the years. This Duesenberg Model J Dual Cowl Phaeton sold at auction for $1,320,000 as long ago as 1990, an unimaginable price at the time. Yet its value continues to rise as when it next came under the hammer, in 2006, it made $3,190,000.

Country of Origin:	USA
Body Design:	LeBaron
Manufacture Date:	1929-37
Power:	265bhp (198kW) @ 4250rpm
Maximum Torque:	374 lb.ft (507Nm) @ 2000rpm
Top Speed:	109mph (175km/h)
0-60mph (0-97km/h):	10.5 secs
Transmission:	3-speed manual
Engine:	420 cu. in (6,882cc) straight eight
Length:	5652mm (222.5 in.)
Width:	1828mm (72 in.)
Wheelbase:	3619mm (142.5 in.)
Kerb Weight:	2390kg (5269 lbs.)
Brakes:	Drums
Suspension:	Beam axle with semi-elliptic springs and hydraulic lever shock absorbers (F); Live axle with semi-elliptic springs and hydraulic lever shock absorbers (R)
Price at Auction:	2006 £2,073,500 (€2,431,099; $3,190,000)

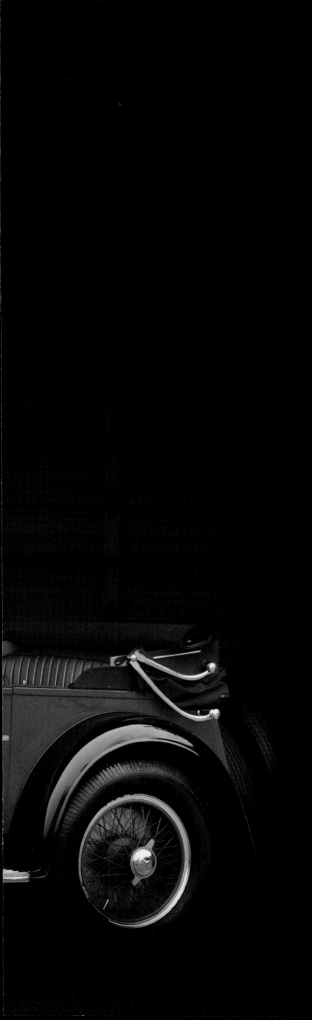

1930 MERCEDES-BENZ SS

It is reported that Mercedes-Benz lost money on every one of around 400 S model cars that it built between 1927 and 1932, but the cars represented for the company the ultimate moving advertisement of its products and its engineering expertise. The company had learned how to supercharge aero engines during the First World War but was banned by the Treaty of Versailles from any further aero engine development or manufacturing. But that knowledge was put to good use when Ferdinand Porsche arrived at the company as Chief Engineer and started to develop a new line of sports cars.

These were the S (for Sport), SS (Supersport) in 1928, SSK (Super Sport Kurz — "Short") from 1929 and SSKL (Super Sport Kurz Leicht — "Short Light") from 1931. The new car immediately showed its pedigree when an early Type S Mercedes won the opening Grand Prix at the recently-opened Nürburgring in 1927 and introduced the spectators to the fierce whine of a highly-stressed supercharged engine.

The engine was increased in size from 6,800cc to 7,065cc for the SS model, in which Rudi Caracciola won the 1928 German Grand Prix in front of the Grand Prix Bugattis, and the 1929 Ulster Tourist Trophy, defeating a team of three 4.5-litre "Blower" Bentleys in the process.

And yet the Mercedes-Benz SS — also known as the 38/250 — was very much in demand as a high-performance road car and it quickly earned a reputation as one of the world's best cars of its day, combining astonishing performance with a style that would be emulated by other manufacturers in the years that followed.

The SS was a little lighter than the S model, and its power output was increased to 200bhp. This was more than enough to provide a top speed of 115mph (185km/h) and acceleration from 0-60mph in under 15 seconds. It doesn't sound much today, but in 1928 that was supercar performance. The majority were offered with a four-seater touring body from the factory but a few were fitted with coachbuilt bodies.

It's believed that 173 SS models were manufactured and although the car nominally remained in production until 1933 in fact the majority were sold before 1930. By that time, Ferdinand Porsche had left Mercedes-Benz after a boardroom tussle but his legacy lives on in a line of magnificent sports cars that combine brute power with understated elegance.

Fine examples rarely come up at auction but a highly original 1930 Mercedes-Benz 38/250 SS Sports Tourer was offered in August 2010 and duly fetched $2,537,000. Some would say that's a small price to pay for such an iconic car.

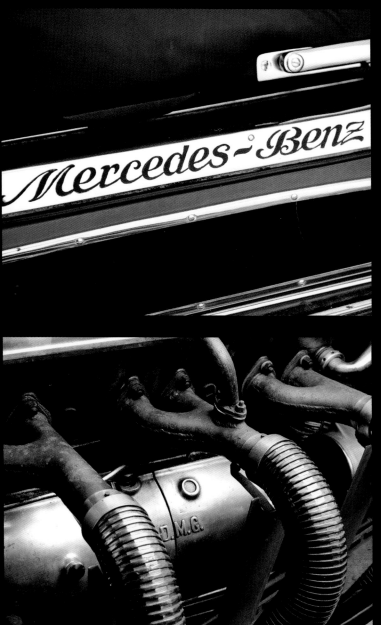

Country of Origin:	Germany
Body Design:	Mercedes-Benz
Manufacture Date:	1928-33
Power:	200bhp (149kW) @ 3400rpm
Maximum Torque:	450Nm (332 lb.ft.)
Top Speed:	115mph (185km/h)
0-60mph (0-97km/h):	15.0 secs
Transmission:	4-speed manual
Engine:	7,065cc straight six
Length:	5200mm (205 in.)
Width:	1700mm (70 in.)
Wheelbase:	3400mm (134 in.)
Kerb Weight:	2268kg (5000 lbs.)
Brakes:	Drums
Suspension:	Live axle, semi-elliptic leaf springs, friction dampers (F); Live axle, semi-elliptic leaf springs, friction dampers (R)
Auction Sale:	2010 £ 1,649,050 (€1,933,447; $2,537,000)

1931 BUGATTI ROYALE TYPE 41

The Bugatti Royale, or Type 41, was intended from the start for kings, queens, emperors and other heads of state. Ettore Bugatti had started thinking about producing a massive luxury car as early as 1913 when he envisaged a car "larger than a Rolls-Royce, but lighter... with a closed body it will reach 150km/h (93mph) and I hope to make it silent ... it will undoubtedly be a car and a piece of machinery beyond all criticism".

The first prototype was built in 1926 and sported an open tourer body from a Packard. Bugatti intended that this would form the basis of a production run of 25 Royales, though the onset of the Great Depression meant that in fact only six were built and of these only three were actually sold.

It was fitted with a strangely-proportioned two door, three seat coupé body in 1928 and with a third body the same year, this time a more elegant four-door saloon, built in the style of a classic carriage.

Seeking a more modern appearance, it was then fitted with a far more elegant two-door body by the Parisian coachbuilder Weymann in 1929. This car was later destroyed in an accident and re-built with a completely new body designed by the young Jean Bugatti. This design, which owed much to the style of Duesenberg cars, was called the "Coupé Napoleon".

At the time it was the world's largest car with a massive 15-litre engine, though the later production cars were fitted with a slightly more modest 12.7-litre straight eight powerplant. It was based on an aero engine design created for the French air force and featured three valves per cylinder though only a single carburettor.

Of the Royale's actually sold, the first went to businessman Armand Esders in 1932, fitted with a beautiful roadster body with no headlamps as Esders had no intention of driving at night. It was later fitted with a Coupe de Ville body by Henry Binder of Paris and was rumoured to have been bought by Volkswagen (the new owners of the Bugatti brand) for around $15,000,000 in 1999.

Other Royales are in the Henry Ford Museum in Detroit and the French National Motor Museum (formerly the Schlumpf collection). Another was sold to the Blackhawk Collection in California for $8,000,000 in 1991. Yet another, a Kellner-bodied coupé, made $8,700,000 at auction in 1983 and was then reportedly sold to the Japanese Meitec Corporation for $15,700,000 in 1990 and this car was later offered for sale by private treaty for £10,000,000 in 2001. Values may have slipped a little since then but a Royale is unlikely to go for under $10,000,000.

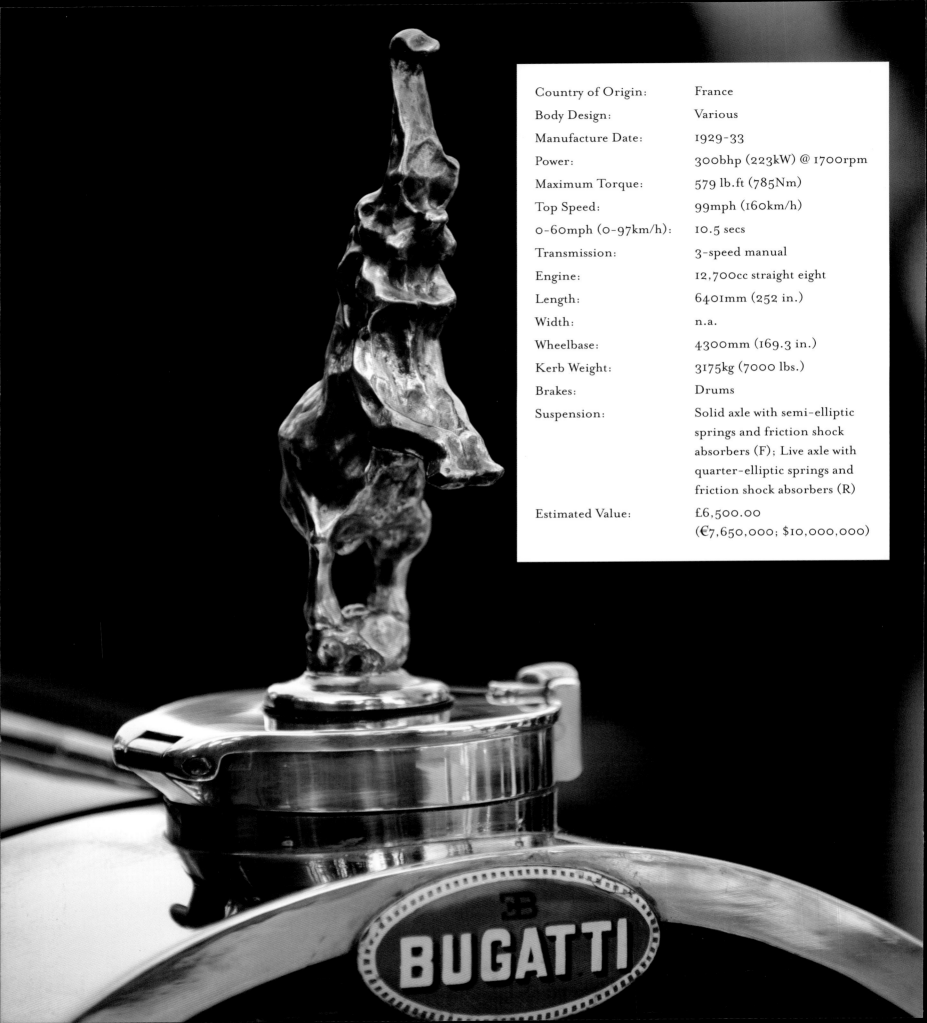

Country of Origin:	France
Body Design:	Various
Manufacture Date:	1929-33
Power:	300bhp (223kW) @ 1700rpm
Maximum Torque:	579 lb.ft (785Nm)
Top Speed:	99mph (160km/h)
0-60mph (0-97km/h):	10.5 secs
Transmission:	3-speed manual
Engine:	12,700cc straight eight
Length:	6401mm (252 in.)
Width:	n.a.
Wheelbase:	4300mm (169.3 in.)
Kerb Weight:	3175kg (7000 lbs.)
Brakes:	Drums
Suspension:	Solid axle with semi-elliptic springs and friction shock absorbers (F); Live axle with quarter-elliptic springs and friction shock absorbers (R)
Estimated Value:	£6,500.00 (€7,650,000; $10,000,000)

1932 BUGATTI TYPE 55

Ettore Bugatti was an automobile genius who created a company with an unrivalled reputation for high performance road and race cars. And when the time came to pass his mantle on to the next generation, his son Jean Bugatti proved that he too was touched by genius.

The Bugatti Type 55 was first introduced in 1931 at the Paris Motor Show, based on the chassis of the Type 54 Grand Prix car and was powered by the 2.3-litre twin overhead cam engine from the Type 51 Grand Prix car fitted with a Zenith carburettor and a Rootes-type supercharger. It was detuned slightly, with a lower compression ratio to make it more driveable and to allow it to run on the standard petrol available to motorists in those days, but still offered a fine turn of performance with contemporary road testers claiming to have extracted a top speed of 112mph (180km/h).

But just as important as the Type 55's performance was its appearance. A number of different bodies were created by independent coachbuilders but of the 38 Type 55 cars built, seven were factory coupés and sixteen sported wonderfully elegant two-seater coachwork designed by Jean Bugatti himself, at the tender age of just 22.

At the front was the traditional Bugatti horseshoe-shaped grille on either side of which was a long flowing wing line that stretched from front to rear in an unbroken line, swooping down at the sides to allow access to the cockpit. It has been suggested that this style provided the inspiration for the lines of the massive Bugatti Royale. One aspect of the design that set the 55 apart was the use of body mouldings tapering along the sides of the bonnet and the boot which allowed Jean Bugatti to adopt a two-tone colour scheme.

This magnificent sports car – often dubbed the most attractive car ever sold – became known as the Type 55 Super Sport and sold in its native France for 72,500 Francs – an enormous sum in the early 1930's. The majority were used by wealthy owners as road cars but some were raced too, including at Le Mans in 1934 when Brunet's Bugatti Type 55 reached fifth place before crashing out of contention. Of the original 38, some 30 are known to survive of which six are owned by the French National Motor Museum. Other examples very rarely come to market, though one example made £1,108,000 at auction in 2003, and another made €2,097,500 at auction in Monaco in 2008.

Country of Origin:	France	Width:	1760mm (69.3 in.)
Body Design:	Jean Bugatti	Wheelbase:	2750mm (108.2 in.)
Manufacture Date:	1931-35	Kerb Weight:	1200kg (2645 lbs.)
Power:	130bhp (95.7kW) @ 5000rpm	Brakes:	Cable-operated drums
Maximum Torque:	129 lb.ft. (175Nm)	Suspension:	Live axe, semi-elliptical
Top Speed:	112mph (180km/h)		leaf springs and friction
0-60mph (0-97km/h):	13 secs		dampers (F); Live axle with
Transmission:	4-speed manual		quarter-elliptic leaf springs
Engine:	2,262cc straight eight		and friction dampers (R)
Length:	4700mm (185 in.)	Auction Sale:	2008 £1,788,971
			(€2,097,500; $2,752,263)

1933 BUGATTI TYPE 59 SUPERCHARGED 3.3 LITRE

Despite being in many ways behind the times – the Bugatti Type 59 Grand Prix car still had solid axles and cable-operated drum brakes at a time when racing rivals were moving to independent suspension and hydraulic braking systems – it was the last successful Bugatti Grand Prix car.

At the outset, the Type 59 was fitted with a 2.8-litre supercharged straight eight engine into what was in essence a shorter wheelbase derivative of the Type 54 chassis.

The new car appeared for the first time in 1933 though with a new 750kg formula being introduced in 1934, the cars had to be modified and weight shed by drilling holes in the chassis. After a number of setbacks, Type 59s managed wins at the hands of Dreyfuss at the Belgian Grand Prix and Wimille at the Algiers Grand Prix in 1934, but Ettore Bugatti withdrew from Grand Prix racing, unable to compete on a level playing field with Alfa Romeo, Mercedes-Benz and Auto Union because the French Government declined to support Bugatti financially in the way that the Italian and German Governments supported their national teams. However, the Type 59's career was not altogether foreshortened because Bugatti sold four works Type 59 cars to privateers in Great Britain and in their hands the Type 59 captured a handful of further Grand prix victories in the following years. Bugatti also sold one of the remaining Type 59s to King Leopold of Belgium.

The Type 59's original 2.8-litre engine, even with the help of its Rootes-type supercharger and twin downdraft Zenith carburettors, was uncompetitive in the face of its main rival, the Alfa Romeo P3. When the stroke was increased from 88 to 100mm and the capacity boosted to 3,257cc the Bugatti 59 was quick enough but sadly unreliable. Its four-speed gearbox, mounted between the engine and the rear axle, in particular was a weak point.

The car certainly looked the business, as elegant as the earlier Type 35 with its horseshoe-shaped radiator, tapering tail, and all-aluminium bodywork. This was also the very first appearance on a Bugatti of 'piano-wire' spoked wheels – a typically elegant Bugatti solution as the wires only were required to support radial loads because an aluminium back-plate coped with the torque loads involved with accelerating and braking.

Bugatti had originally planned to build 12 Type 59 chassis, though only eight examples appeared to have been built and five are known to survive. The last to appear at auction, in 2005, achieved a top bid of £1,321,500 despite being a non-runner.

Country of Origin:	France
Body Design:	Bugatti
Manufacture Date:	1933-36
Power:	250bhp (187kW) @ 5500rpm
Maximum Torque:	n.a.
Top Speed:	159mph (256km/h)
0-60mph (0-97km/h):	n.a.
Transmission:	4-speed manual
Engine:	3,257cc straight eight
Length:	3744mm (147.4 in.)
Width:	1630mm (64.2 in.)
Wheelbase:	2597mm (102.2 in.)
Kerb Weight:	748kg (1649 lbs.)
Brakes:	Cable operated drums
Suspension:	Solid axe, semi-elliptical leaf springs and de Ram shock absorbers (F); Live axle with reversed quarter-elliptic leaf springs and de Ram shock absorbers (R)
Auction Sale:	2005 £1,321,500 (€1,549,407; $2,033,076)

1933 DUESENBERG MODEL SJ PHAETON

The Duesenberg brothers, Augie and Fred, starting building racing cars then in 1920 launched their first road car, the Model A. They made and sold around 600 examples before their company was bought by Errett Lobban Cord. Cord had made a success of Auburn and now encouraged the Duesenbergs to create America's finest car, money no object.

It first appeared in December 1928 at the New York Auto Show when a sleek and powerful Duesenberg J model was unveiled. It had a massive 420 cu. in. straight eight engine built by the aircraft manufacturer Lycoming which featured two overhead camshafts and four valves per cylinder, providing a claimed output of 265bhp at 4,250rpm — which made it twice as powerful as any other car on the market at that time.

It was an immediate success, particularly with Hollywood stars such as Gary Cooper, Clark Gable, Greta Garbo and Mae West, all of whom were customers. The Duesenberg brothers had succeeded in creating one of the world's finest and most opulent cars but its performance was less than spectacular because of the car's massive size and weight.

The answer came in the form of a centrifugal supercharger which boosted power to 320bhp and performance into what was the supercar league in its day. This supercharged model was called the SJ, instantly recognisable thanks to its chromed exhaust headers protruding from the side of the engine.

Like the Duesenberg J, the SJ was sold as a running chassis to which buyers added a body created by one of a number of coachbuilding firms. Duesenberg themselves offered bodies under the name of Le Grande though the coachbuilding work was put out to other firms. Because of this arrangement, there are both long and short wheelbase SJ models, each with a variety of bodywork styles.

For many, the most elegant Duesenberg SJ's are those on a long wheelbase. Only around 36 Duesenberg SJ's were ever built, of which 18 were the long wheelbase variety. Rarer still are the long wheelbase Le Grande Phaeton models, as only three were made.

When the first Duesenberg SJ was sold in 1932 the chassis alone cost $8,000 and this had gone up to $10,000 by 1935, when the last SJ was built. Add the cost of coachbuilding and this represented an astronomical sum in those days, one reason perhaps why the Cord, Auburn and Duesenberg brands all collapsed in 1937 during a time of widespread economic hardship. Today, the Duesenberg SJ's value is once again stratospheric, with a pristine example reaching $1,688,500 in 2008.

Country of Origin:	USA
Body Design:	Gordon Buehrig
Manufacture Date:	1932-35
Power:	320bhp (239kW) @ 4200rpm
Maximum Torque:	425 lb.ft (576Nm) @ 2400rpm
Top Speed:	130mph (209km/h)
0-60mph (0-97km/h):	8.5 secs
Transmission:	3-speed manual
Engine:	420 cu. in (6,882cc) straight eight
Length:	5652mm (222.5 in.)
Width:	1828mm (72 in.)
Wheelbase:	3619mm (142.5 in.)
Kerb Weight:	2268kg (5000 lbs.)
Brakes:	Drums
Suspension:	Beam axle with leaf springs and shock absorbers (F); Live axle with leaf springs and shock absorbers (R)
Auction Sale:	2008 £1,097,525 (€1,286,805; $1,688,500)

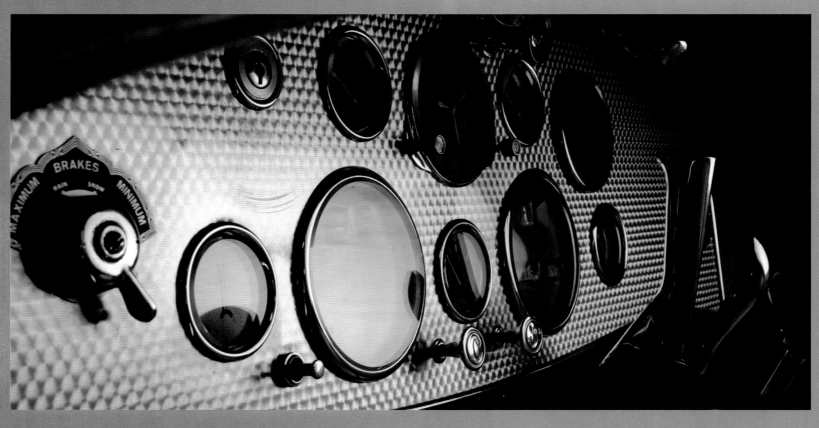

1934 PACKARD 12 RUNABOUT LEBARON SPEEDSTER

From the time the very first Packard was built in 1899, the watchword was quality. James Ward Packard of Warren Ohio was unhappy with the car he had bought so, with the help of his brother, he decided to build his own.

They built a fine car but the Packards didn't stay long in the business. Nevertheless their company survived as a luxury car builder and it was Packard that introduced the world's first production 12-cylinder engine in 1915. A new straight-eight powerplant superseded the V12 in 1923 and for a while the company concentrated on smaller cars — which helped it survive the Great Depression — but by 1932 it was felt that the time was right for another top-of-the-range V12. The new flagship was called the "Twin Six" initially but very soon it gained a new name — the Packard Twelve.

It was not the fastest car on the market but it quickly gained a reputation for being the quietest and smoothest that money could buy. It was also one of the easiest to drive because, although other manufacturers offered power-assisted braking and clutch systems, only Packard also offered a power-assisted gear change.

The car was offered in two standard chassis lengths — 3610mm (142 inches) or 3730mm (147 inches), to which a number of different bodies could be fitted. Some Packard Twelves were sold direct from the factory with standard bodies, but many of the 5,700 examples built between 1932 and 1939 when the Twelve finally went out of production, were ordered with bodywork by the finest American coachbuilding forms such as Dietrich and LeBaron.

One of those coachbuilt Packard Twelves was truly special — the Runabout Speedster built by LeBaron. It was set apart by its elegant pontoon fenders, elongated bonnet and smoothly tapered boat-tail rear. In addition, it was built on a shorter (3429mm, 135 inches) chassis normally reserved for 8-cylinder cars. The Runabout Speedster also used the 8-cylinder's much lighter axles, wheels, brakes and transmission which, when mated with the V12, provided the highest power to weight ratio of any Packard car. It was also extremely rare — just four were built and each is slightly different in detail — and its $7,260 price tag was as much as a luxury yacht might have cost in those days.

All Packard cars have a reputation for being built to the highest possible standard, but the Runabout Speedster is different because many observers reckon this is the most elegant Packard ever built, and perhaps the most beautiful American coachbuilt car of all time. No wonder that when one was offered at auction in 2006 it made over $3,000,000.

Country of Origin:	USA
Body Design:	Alex Tremulis
Manufacture Date:	1940-41
Power:	160bhp (119kW) @ 3200rpm
Maximum Torque:	322 lb.ft (437Nm) @ 1400rpm
Top Speed:	90mph (145km/h)
0-60mph (0-97km/h):	n.a.
Transmission:	3-speed synchromesh manual
Engine:	445 cu. in (7,292cc) V12
Length:	n.a.
Width:	1346mm (53 in.)
Wheelbase:	3429mm (135 in.)
Kerb Weight:	2495kg (5500 lbs.)
Brakes:	Drums
Suspension:	Rigid axle, semi-elliptic springs (F); Live axle (R)
Price at Auction/ Private Sale:	£2,073,500 (€2,431,099; $3,190,000)

1935 DUESENBERG SJ SPEEDSTER MORMON METEOR

John Cobb in his Railton Special, Sir Malcolm Campbell in Bluebird and Captain George Eyston in Thunderbolt all gained fame as early British holders of the land speed record. And one man they have to thank for those successes is American businessman Ab Jenkins who was one of the very first to recognise the potential of the Bonneville Salt Flats for record runs and who worked tirelessly to persuade the British LSR contenders to switch their attentions from Daytona Beach in Florida to Bonneville in Utah.

Ab Jenkins started setting records at Bonneville in 1925 when he challenged the Union Pacific Railroad to a race across the flats from Wendover to Salt Lake City. Later he started setting 24-hour records, achieving an average of 127.229mph (204.755km/h) in 1934. For good measure he reached a terrifying 68mph (109km/h) on an Allis-Chambers farm tractor the following year.

The tractor was a diversion because Ab's serious project for 1935 involved a Duesenberg Special, essentially a standard 142-in. wheelbase Duesenberg J chassis with a bespoke aerodynamic body designed by Herbert Newport.

Duesenberg supplied a pair of modified engines based on the supercharged SJ unit but with hotter cams, and two massive duplex Bendix-Stromberg carburettors to boost the power output to 400bhp. But apart from this, there was very little to distinguish the Duesenberg Special from a standard Duesenberg car.

After a couple of hiccups — special new bearings had to be fitted and on one attempt the crankcase split — Ab Jenkins and his Duesenberg Special had broken a whole host of records including achieving an astonishing 3,253 miles in 24 hours at an average speed of 135.47mph (218km/h).

There was more to come. For the 1936 record season Jenkins fitted a massive 1,750cu in. Curtiss Conquerer V12 into the Duesenberg's chassis and re-named it Mormon Meteor.

That year, Cobb, Eyston and Jenkins were all at Bonneville and the 24-hour record yo-yoed between them; but in the end it was the Mormon Meteor that was the fastest, raising the record to 153.823mph (247.554km/h).

Jenkins continued to set records but later re-fitted the Duesenberg SJ engine into the chassis and used the car as a moving billboard in his successful attempt to be elected mayor of Salt Lake City.

It's a unique car, a genuine 24-hour land speed record holder and unquestionably the fastest, most powerful and most famous of all the Duesenberg SJ's. When it came up for auction in 2004 it made $4,455,000, then the highest price ever paid for an American car.

Country of Origin:	USA
Body Design:	Herbert Newport
Manufacture Date:	1935
Power:	400bhp (298kW) @ 5000rpm
Maximum Torque:	n.a.
Top Speed:	160mph (258km/h)
0-60mph (0-97km/h):	n.a.
Transmission:	3-speed manual
Engine:	420 cu. in (6,882cc) straight eight
Length:	5652mm (222.5 in.)
Width:	1828mm (72 in.)
Wheelbase:	3619mm (142.5 in.)
Kerb Weight:	2177kg (4800 lbs.)
Brakes:	Drums
Suspension:	Beam axle with leaf springs and shock absorbers (F); Live axle with leaf springs and shock absorbers (R)
Auction Sale:	2004 £2,895,750 (€3,395,156; $4,455,000)

1935 DUESENBERG SJN CONVERTIBLE COUPÉ

Frederick and August Duesenberg were brothers with an innate love of high-quality craftsmanship and fine engineering. They not only produced some of the world's most expensive cars — since the price inevitably reflected the standards of workmanship that went into the automotive works of art that bore the Duesenberg name — but they also produced some of the world's fastest. It was, after all, a 16-litre Duesenberg that lifted the land speed record to 159mph (254km/h at Daytona Beach in 1919; and it was also a Duesenberg that was the only American manufactured car ever to win a Grand Prix when Jimmy Murphy won the French GP at Le Mans in 1921. The following year, eight of the top 10 finishers at the Indianapolis 500 were powered by Duesenberg engines, including the winner's — Jimmy Murphy again.

Had the brothers invested as much time and energy into their commercial affairs, it's possible their company may have been able to remain independent, but in 1926 they were forced to sell out to E.L.Cord. Cord's vision was for Duesenberg to produce the world's greatest car, surpassing even the likes of Rolls-Royce, Bugatti and Cadillac.

That vision came to reality with the Duesenberg SJ which created a sensation when it was first unveiled at the 1928 New York Motor Show. Customers' cars were delivered from 1929 and the combination of massive performance from its 6,882cc straight eight engine together with the finest luxury interiors made this the car of choice for Hollywood stars, business moguls and heads of state.

Far from sitting on its laurels, Duesenberg upped the ante still further in 1932 with the launch of the SJ model. Adding a supercharger boosted the power output to an unimaginable 320bhp, which was enough to allow the 2-tonne car to accelerate to 104mph (167km/h) in second gear, and on to a top speed of 140mph (225km/h).

All Duesenbergs were sold as running chassis to which buyers added a body at often considerable extra cost. One of the more special body options was designed by Herb Newport and built by Rollston in New York. It had a wider than standard body that extended down below the chassis frame rails to give the car a lower profile. Skirted front bumpers and an extended rear deck hiding the fuel tank completed what was an elegant and powerful-looking design.

Only 10 of these so-called 'JN' models were produced, of which just one was supercharged. This makes the SJN Duesenberg literally unique.

Country of Origin:	USA
Body Design:	Rollston
Manufacture Date:	1932-35
Power:	320bhp (239kW) @ 4200rpm
Maximum Torque:	425 lb.ft (576Nm) @ 2400rpm
Top Speed:	140mph (225km/h)
0-60mph (0-97km/h):	8.5 secs
Transmission:	3-speed manual
Engine:	420 cu. in (6,882cc) straight eight
Length:	5652mm (222.5 in.)
Width:	1828mm (72 in.)
Wheelbase:	3619mm (142.5 in.)
Kerb Weight:	2268kg (5000 lbs.)
Brakes:	Drums
Suspension:	Beam axle with leaf springs and shock absorbers (F); Live axle with leaf springs and shock absorbers (R).
Price at Auction:	2004 £6,768,141 (€7,941,035; $10,435,000)

1935 MERCEDES-BENZ 500K SPECIAL ROADSTER

The Mercedes-Benz flagship 500K was first introduced in 1934, a car designed from the outset to be one of the very finest in the world. It was powered by a 5-litre straight eight engine producing 100bhp in normal driving and up to 160bhp when its Rootes-type supercharger was operating with its characteristic whine. It was also that supercharger that gave the car its name because the 'K' stands for 'Kompressor'.

Because of the sheer weight of the massive car, its performance was, in truth, fairly average, but this was something that was taken care of a couple of years later when the 5.4-litre 180bhp 540K model was introduced. Later still, Mercedes-Benz engineers prepared a 580K model, in which the engine was bored out to 5.8-litres to produce 130bhp in normal use and a hefty 200bhp when the driver operated the supercharger; but this model never saw the light of day due to the outbreak of war in 1939.

But it was never supposed to be sheer performance that elevated the 500K over its competitors. It was the comfort, the ease of driving and the sheer style and elegance that truly set it apart. The 500K had fully independent suspension, first introduced by Mercedes-Benz on the 380 model in 1933, but still a rarity in those days. The gearbox featured synchromesh on all but first gear on the standard four-speed and more desirable five-speed transmission options. And even if acceleration was leisurely, the 500K was still good for a top speed of some 100mph (161km/h), even though fuel consumption at those speeds was around 10mpg.

The well-heeled 500K customer could choose from a number of variants including three different chassis variants and a number of different closed and open body styles. But perhaps the most desirable of all was the strictly two-seater Special Roadster, designed in-house by Hermann Ahrens at the Sindelfingen works.

Since only 29 Special Roadsters were built, they are also extremely rare. In 1989 an unrestored example made £1,000,000, then in 2001 a concours-winning Special Roadster sold for $2,970,000 and slightly more recently bidding for yet another reached $2,275,000 though it remained unsold. It's a car that at the time sold new for the same sort of money that an average house might cost. Many were hidden like other valuables during WW2 to protect them from damage and theft, and since then values have continued to appreciate because very few other cars share the 500K Special Roadster's essential qualities of luxury, technological excellence, style and sheer beauty.

Country of Origin:	Germany
Body Design:	Hermann Ahrens
Manufacture Date:	1934-39
Power:	160bhp (119kW) @ 3400rpm
Maximum Torque:	n.a.
Top Speed:	100mph (161km/h)
0-60mph (0-97km/h):	19.0 secs
Transmission:	4-speed manual
Engine:	5,019cc straight eight
Length:	5100mm (200.8 in.)
Width:	1880mm (74.6 in.)
Wheelbase:	3290mm (129.5 in.)
Kerb Weight:	2500kg (5512 lbs.)
Brakes:	Drums
Suspension:	Double wishbones with coil springs and hydraulic shock absorbers (F); Swing axles with trailing arms, coil springs and hydraulic shock absorbers (R).
Auction Sale:	2001 £1,926,342 (€2,260,170; $2,970,000

1936 MERCEDES-BENZ 540K CABRIOLET A

After the success of the supercharged Mercedes-Benz S, SS, SSK and SSKL series cars, what could the Stuttgart-based company do to find a suitable replacement? The answer came in the form of the 500K that was first unveiled at the Berlin Motor Show of 1934, and the 540K which was revealed at the Paris Motor Show of 1936.

A number of different body styles were offered, each of which was distinguished not only by a whole new level of beauty and elegance, but also by their enormous cost. At a time when a Mercedes 4-door 230 saloon cost some 6,000 Reichmarks, the majority of the 500K variants cost between 22,000 and 24,000 Reichmarks and the flagship Special Roadster cost nearer 30,000 Reichmarks.

These were cars for the very wealthiest customers and despite the clouds of war building up, it seemed there were plenty of them – 342 examples of the 500K and a further 319 of the 540K were sold, including a batch of 20 armoured versions for the use of the Nazi high command.

Of all the variants, one of the finer was the 540K Cabriolet A (four different cabriolet body styles were offered, designated A to D). The elongated two seater car featured a 500K body but with the substantially more powerful engine of the 540K.

That engine was a legend in its day, a 5,401cc straight eight with laterally operated valves and a horizontally mounted gear-driven Rootes-type supercharger. This did not operate all the time, but when the accelerator pedal was pushed to the floor it provided a massive extra power boost, up from some 115bhp naturally aspirated to a blown 180bhp.

To ensure the power was suitably controlled, the suspension of the 540K was uprated too. Unusually for that time, it was fully independent, featuring double wishbones and coil springs at the front and trailing arms with coil springs at the rear.

The body was long, low and seductively beautiful, with two headlamps and a distinctive central fog light, low windshield, flowing wings and thoughtful features such as a mud scraper built in to the side step. The spare wheel could either be mounted on the rear boot lid (from which it could be removed without tools), or on the wing (in which case a rear view mirror was mounted on top).

The 540K Cabriolet A is one of the classic pre-war German cars, of which it's believed just 12 examples are still in existence, so it came as no surprise when bidding reached €1,220,000 at auction in 2007.

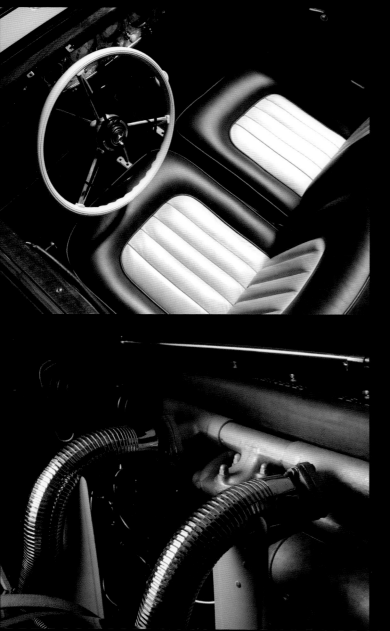

Country of Origin:	Germany
Body Design:	Mercedes-Benz
Manufacture Date:	1936-39
Power:	180bhp (183kW) @ 3400rpm
Maximum Torque:	n.a.
Top Speed:	106mph (170km/h)
0-60mph (0-97km/h):	17.0 secs
Transmission:	4-speed manual
Engine:	5,401cc straight eight
Length:	5100mm (200.8 in.)
Width:	1880mm (74.6 in.)
Wheelbase:	3290mm (129.5 in.)
Kerb Weight	2240kg (4938 lbs.)
Brakes:	Drums
Suspension:	Double wishbones with coil springs and hydraulic shock absorbers (F); Swing axles with trailing arms, coil springs and hydraulic shock absorbers (R).
Auction Sale:	2007 £1,039,805 (€1,220,000; $1,603,153)

1937 ALFA ROMEO 8C 2900 B CABRIOLET

The Alfa Romeo company had enjoyed a glittering early career but had to be rescued from bankruptcy in 1932 by the Italian Government. In terms of payback, President Mussolini made clear that Alfa's job henceforth would be to build high-quality aero engines, to earn prestige for the country by winning at the top level of motor sports, and to use whatever small spare production capacity there might be to built impressively exotic motor cars.

Sure enough, those pre-war years saw the development of the most powerful, elegant and seductive Alfa Romeo cars ever built. At the time Alfa development was under the control of Vittorio Jano, a brilliant engine and chassis engineer who also had a clear vision of the car's body construction and appearance.

Development of the 8C 2300 had started in 1930 and the first example of this classic road racer was entered in the 1931 Mille Miglia. By 1934, some 207 examples had been sold with various bodies designed either for the racetrack or the road, and there is no doubt that this was the model that truly enhanced the purebred reputation of the Alfa Romeo marque.

Despite this, Jano reckoned the 8C 2300 was too heavy to be considered his finest work. But what followed was, by any standards, truly a masterpiece. In 1936 the 8C 2900 A was introduced as a slightly detuned two-seater version of the P3 Grand Prix car. It still produced some 220bhp however, and with the car's weight kept down to just 850kg, it had outstanding performance – more than enough to take the first three places at the 1936 Mille Miglia.

The Mille Miglia cars were basically open-wheel racers with mudguards and lights added but the same basic chassis was used for genuine road cars in 1937. For 1939 the 8C 2900 B was launched, with the engine detuned again to 180bhp but now with fabulously elegant and luxurious bodies by Pininfarina and Touring.

They cost a small fortune at the time – 7,500 lire or the equivalent of $3,945 – but these were the ultimate Alfas and they have more than retained their value to this day. Small wonder that it's an 8C 2900 B that attracted the highest ever bid for an Alfa Romeo of $4,072,500 at the 1999 Christie's auction at Pebble Beach.

One of only 44 cars built on the P3 GP chassis (and one of only 20 8C 2900 Bs), this rare example started life as a cycle-fendered racer owned and raced by Piero Dusio, who later founded Cisitalia, but was later fitted with the Pininfarina Cabriolet body that it still sports today.

Country of Origin:	Italy
Body Design:	Pininfarina
Manufacture Date:	1937-39
Power:	180bhp (134.2kW) @ 5200rpm
Maximum Torque:	n.a.
Top Speed:	109mph (175km/h)
0-60mph (0-97km/h):	11.0 secs
Transmission:	4-speed manual
Engine:	2,905cc straight eight
Length:	4600mm (181.1 in.)
Width:	1668mm (65.7 in.)
Wheelbase:	3000mm (118.1 in.)
Kerb Weight:	1250kg (2750 lbs.)
Brakes:	Drums
Suspension:	Double wishbones with coil springs and hydraulic shock absorbers (F); Swing axles with radius arms, transverse leaf springs and hydraulic and friction shock absorbers (R).
Auction Sale:	£2,641,423 (€3,099,172; $4,072,500)

1937 BUGATTI TYPE 57S

Perhaps the most celebrated non-racing Bugatti ever produced was the Type 57, first introduced in 1934, and which was, for Bugatti, a relatively high volume model with around 710 built before production ceased in 1938.

The Type 57 was designed from the outset to compete with the best that Europe could offer in those days – from manufacturers such as Bentley, Delahaye and Delage. It was powered by Bugatti's 3.3 litre twin-cam straight eight engine producing 140bhp at 4,800rpm. The four-speed manual gearbox was integral with the crankcase and featured a single plate clutch. An independent front suspension system was proposed but the company's founder Ettore Bugatti vetoed such a radical design.

In fact the power output of the standard engine provided fairly modest performance by Bugatti standards – a top speed of only around 90mph (145km/h) – so in 1935 a more powerful 57S model was introduced with a shorter chassis to reduce weight and a tuned engine with a dry sump and a higher compression ratio that boosted the maximum output to 185bhp. Interestingly, the chassis of the 57C was not just shorter than standard but also lower, which meant that the rear axle actually ran through the frame.

Later, in 1937, Bugatti was to introduce a still more powerful derivative, the supercharged Type 57SC in which power was upped once again, to 220bhp. In fact many standard 57S cars were subsequently converted to supercharged specification.

What truly set the Type 57 apart was the work of Jean Bugatti – son of Ettore Bugatti – who was responsible for the coachwork. For the Type 57 Bugatti offered a number of different bodywork options including the 4-door Galibier, and the 2 door Ventoux, Atalanté, Stelvio and Atlantic (the famous model built using aircraft-style riveted joints).

Only 17 Type 57S Atalanté cars were built, which makes it a rare example of the Bugatti breed. One particular 57S is even rarer as it was bought new from the factory in 1937 by Lord Howe (who successfully raced a Bugatti T57). He drove the car for eight years before selling it on and a later owner, Harold Carr, bought it in 1955 for £895. A few years later he locked it in his garage where it remained untouched and unused until his death in 2007 after which his nephew re-discovered the "barn find of the century".

The Earl Howe Bugatti Type 57S was auctioned by Bonhams at the 2009 Retromobile car show with a reserve of £3 million, though there was speculation that it might reach double that figure. In the event it was sold for €3,417,500.

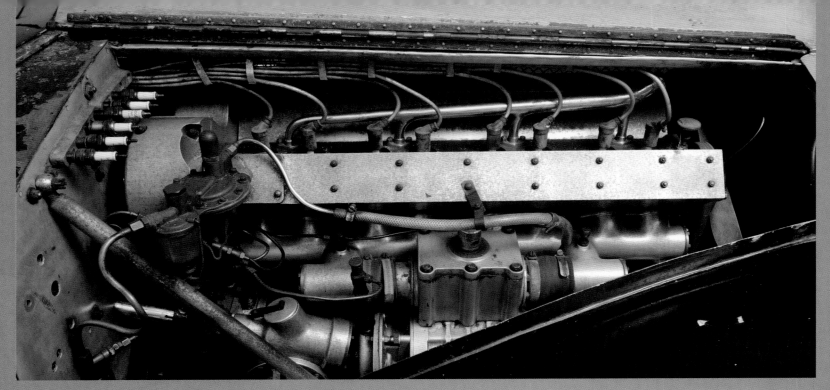

Country of Origin:	France
Body Design:	Jean Bugatti
Manufacture Date:	1934-38
Power:	175bhp (130kW) @ 5500rpm
Maximum Torque:	n.a.
Top Speed:	130mph (209km/h)
0-60mph (0-97km/h):	10.0 secs
Transmission:	4-speed manual
Engine:	3,257cc straight eight
Length:	4600mm (181 in.)
Width:	1760mm (69.3 in.)
Wheelbase:	2980mm (117.3 in.)
Kerb Weight:	1550kg (3417 lbs.)
Brakes:	Hydraulic drums
Suspension:	Beam axe, semi-elliptical leaf springs and de Ram shock absorbers (F); Live axle with reversed quarter-elliptic leaf springs and de Ram shock absorbers (R).
Auction Sale:	2009 £2,912,734 (€3,417,500; $4,490,802)

1937 MERCEDES-BENZ 540K SPECIAL ROADSTER

Mercedes-Benz had created a tradition of magnificent supercharged cars with the S, SSK and SSKL models built between 1927 and 1934. These cars were driven by politicians, film stars and business leaders around the world so developing a suitable replacement was no simple task.

Yet Mercedes managed not just to create an eminently suitable replacement, but one which surpassed all that had gone before. At the 1934 Berlin Motor Show the company unveiled its 500K model, with 100bhp in standard form and 160bhp when supercharged. Two years later at the Paris Show the 540K was launched with a larger engine producing 115bhp or 180bhp when supercharged. The 540K also had a longer wheelbase which improved the ride

Numerous different body styles were offered, including saloons, tourers, coupés and cabriolets and once again the world's rich and famous made this their vehicle of choice – including one Indian Maharajah who used his from which to hunt tigers.

But perhaps the most desirable of all the 540K variants was the Special Roadster which cost 6,000 Reichmarks more than the 22,000 Reichmarks that most other models cost at the time. To put this into perspective, the US importer charged $14,000 for a Special Roadster at a time when the most expensive Cadillac V16 was selling for around $8,500.

Despite its enormous bulk and length, the 540K Special Roadster was strictly a two-seater, one designed and built not so much for out-and-out sports car performance but for relaxed high-speed long-distance touring in the ultimate luxury and comfort. If an extra burst of speed was required the driver could operate the supercharger to boost the engine's power output by 60% for short periods.

The 540K also featured independent suspension, a synchromesh gearbox, vacuum-assisted brakes and 12-volt electrics, all of which were state-of-the-art in the mid-1930s. However, few other models shared one the 540K's most outstanding features — the two massive exhausts that are routed from the engine out of the right-hand side of the bonnet before disappearing into the wing. In size, appearance and performance the 540K was a truly impressive performer.

Because of its cost and exclusivity, the 540K was inevitable built in modest numbers — just 319 were built before production ended when war broke out in 1939. Of these, the Special Tourer is truly a rarity as only 26 of these exceptional cars were made. The 540K cost a small fortune when new but it has more than retained its value as the most recent example to come up for auction reached an amazing £3,905,000.

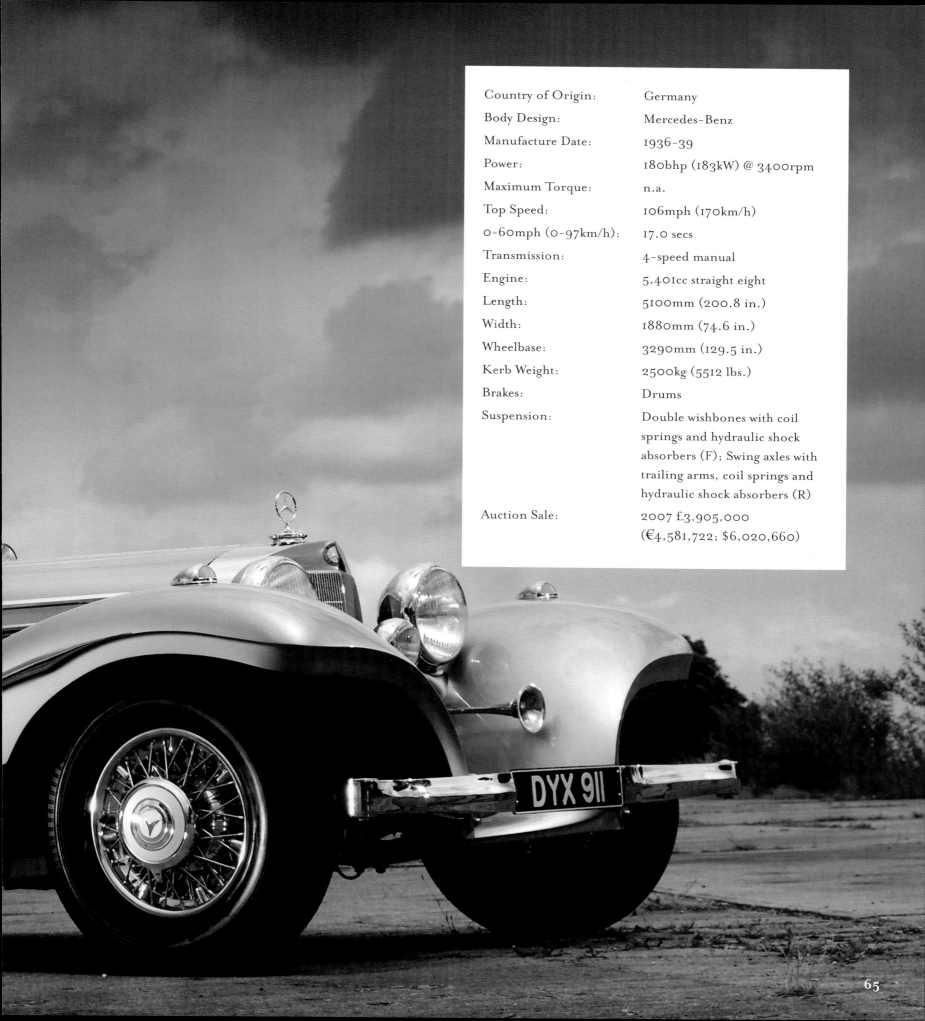

Country of Origin:	Germany
Body Design:	Mercedes-Benz
Manufacture Date:	1936-39
Power:	180bhp (183kW) @ 3400rpm
Maximum Torque:	n.a.
Top Speed:	106mph (170km/h)
0-60mph (0-97km/h):	17.0 secs
Transmission:	4-speed manual
Engine:	5,401cc straight eight
Length:	5100mm (200.8 in.)
Width:	1880mm (74.6 in.)
Wheelbase:	3290mm (129.5 in.)
Kerb Weight:	2500kg (5512 lbs.)
Brakes:	Drums
Suspension:	Double wishbones with coil springs and hydraulic shock absorbers (F); Swing axles with trailing arms, coil springs and hydraulic shock absorbers (R)
Auction Sale:	2007 £3,905,000 (€4,581,722; $6,020,660)

1938 ALFA ROMEO 8C
TIPO 2900 B

The Alfa Romeo 8C 2900 B, introduced in 1937, was the supercar of its time. Developed from the earlier 8C 2900 A which had shown its class by taking the first three places at the 1936 Mille Miglia, the 2900 B was bigger and heavier but it combined the power afforded by a racing engine with twin superchargers with a sophisticated chassis with fully independent suspension clothed in what were some of the most beautiful and elegant car bodies ever produced.

The car was produced in very small numbers on either long (Lungo) or short (Corto) wheelbases, and with a variety of bodies, closed and open, some by Alfa Romeo but the majority by Touring of Milan or Pininfarina.

At the heart of the 8C 2900 B was a magnificent straight eight alloy engine with hemispherical combustion chambers and a dry sump. It was developed from Alfa Romeo's chief designer Vittorio Jano's 2.3-litre straight eight from the early 1930's and was, in effect, a competition car engine detuned to make it a little more tractable on the road. To improve the weight distribution, Jano positioned the four-speed transmission at the rear with the differential. It was not the car's only innovation, because it was one of only a handful of cars at that time to feature independent suspension. By today's standards the swing-axle set up is rather crude but at the time it provided outstanding roadholding.

Production of the 8C 2900 B ended prematurely with the outbreak of war in 1939 and by that time just 10 long wheelbase and 20 short wheelbase cars had been built.

Of these, perhaps the most desirable are those clothed with Touring's 'Superleggera" or ultra-light bodies. Touring created the frame using a technology developed by Zagato, which employed thin metal tubing that was both light and strong. Over this was fitted a slim and supremely elegant body that has been described as one of the world's most beautiful. For its time it was also impressively aerodynamic.

This chassis number 412019 stands out because it was the last short wheelbase car to be fitted with Touring's spider coachwork. Originally sold to the Maharajah of Indore, it was later sold to an Australian and it remained in Australia until 1969. It came to the USA where it passed through various hands before being fully restored. Eventually it arrived in fashion designer Ralph Lauren's collection. It was then sold to a private collector for a reported $10,000,000 in 2004.

Country of Origin:	Italy
Body Design:	Touring
Manufacture Date:	1937-39
Power:	180bhp (134.2 kW) @ 5200rpm
Maximum Torque:	n.a.
Top Speed:	115mph (185 km/h)
0-60 mph (0-97 km/h):	9.6 secs
Transmission:	4-speed manual
Engine:	2,905cc straight eight
Length:	4185mm (174.4 in.)
Width:	1668mm (65.7 in.)
Wheelbase:	2800mm (110.2 in.)
Kerb Weight:	1150kg (2530 lbs.)
Brakes:	Drum brakes
Suspension:	Double wishbones with coil springs and hydraulic shock absorbers (F); Swing axles with radius arms, transverse leaf springs and hydraulic and friction shock absorbers (R)
Private Treaty Sale:	2004 £6,287,000 (€7,522,000; $10,000,000)

1938 DELAHAYE 135 MS COMPETITION CABRIOLET

The Delahaye started life in 1845 as a supplier of ceramics manufacturing machinery in France but later in the century it started making static engines and then automobiles. The finest creation of the company is generally believed to be the 135 model that was first launched at the 1935 Paris Motor Show and which immediately showed its performance potential. As a result, the company quickly introduced a 135 sport model with even greater power and performance.

Two different versions of the sporty but elegant cars were offered: the Delahaye 135 M which was fitted with a single Solex Carburettor) and the more potent 135 MS (which stands for Modifiée Spéciale), whose triple carburettors and larger valves boosted power output to as much as 160bhp and the top speed to 110mph (177km/h). It also had an advanced chassis with independent front suspension and a low centre of gravity which ensured good handling and roadholding.

Buyers could choose between a four-speed manual or a four-speed Cotal semi-automatic transmission. Bodywork of the majority of these cars was by Figoni et Falaschi though Dalahaye 135s were also bodied by other coachmakers such as Saoutchik and Letourneur et Marchand.

This was a car that was both supremely elegant and one of the fastest vehicles available at the time. As a result the Delahaye won numerous competition laurels, dominating French sports car racing in the 1930's, acquitting itself well at Le Mans and even proving itself to be the fastest car in Britain in 1938 at a competition held at Brooklands.

The price of the 135 MS was inevitably high — the equivalent of over $5,000 in those pre-war days — but the Delahaye 135 was a considerable commercial success, with some 1155 examples sold between 1935 and 1952 when it was eventually replaced by the Delahaye 235 model.

The Delahaye 135 is now a highly sought-after collector's car, with the finest examples fetching between $1.5 and $2 million dollars. One particularly fine example made €1,790,000 at a recent RM Auction in Monaco, a 135 MS Cabriolet with bodywork by Figoni et Falaschi that was ordered in 1938 with a custom-fitted interior by the famous French saddlery firm Hermès. When the car was the subject of a full restoration, Hermès supplied new leather for the interior and made up a new set of custom luggage.

Country of Origin:	France
Body Design:	Figoni et Falaschi
Manufacture Date:	1935-52
Power:	160bhp (119kW) @ 4000rpm
Maximum Torque:	n.a.
Top Speed:	110mph (177km/h)
0-60mph (0-97km/h):	14.0 secs
Transmission:	4-speed semi-automatic
Engine:	3,557cc straight six
Length:	n.a.
Width:	n.a.
Wheelbase:	2700mm (106 in.)
Kerb Weight:	1398kg (3,080 lbs.)
Brakes:	Drums
Suspension:	Independent with semi-elliptic springs and friction dampers (F); Live axle with leaf springs and friction dampers (R)
Auction Sale:	2010 £1,525,616 (€1,790,000; $2,352,168)

1938 TALBOT LAGO T23 TEARDROP COUPÉ

The Sunbeam-Talbot-Darracq group became part of the British Rootes Group in the 1920s, but one small part of the former French automobile empire remained independent — the Talbot factory at Suresnes in Paris was sold to the Italian-born businessman Tony Lago.

He then set his chief engineer Walter Becchia to work to create a new 4-litre car, based on the earlier Talbot T120, for entry into sports car events. This Grand Sport Talbot-Lago Special was completed in time for the 1936 French Sports Car Grand Prix at Montlhéry and even though lead driver René Dreyfus managed to get the fastest lap, he finished well back in the field.

That same year, 1936, a road going version — the T150 Lago Special - was launched at the Paris Motor Show, clothed in a two door body. Its six-cylinder engine featured triple carburettors and hemispherical combustion chambers and drive was transmitted to the rear wheels via a Wilson four-speed pre-selector gearbox (since Lago held the foreign rights to this British transmission).

The following year, the Talbot-Lago Special took first, second and third places at the French Grand Prix and first and second at the Tourist Trophy at Donington.

Perhaps by way of celebration, Lago invited the best of the Parisien coachbuilders — Pourtout, Saoutchik and Figoni & Falaschi — to create new bodies for the road-going T150 chassis. The latter's coupé design featured not a single straight line and was quickly dubbed Goutte d'Eau or "Teardrop". To most eyes, it was a strikingly beautiful design though Jaguar founder Sir William Lyons is quoted as describing it as "positively indecent".

Indecent or not, it was certainly very effective aerodynamically as a Teardrop Talbot-Lago acquitted itself well, coming third at Le Mans in 1938 thanks in part to the high speeds achieved on the long Mulsanne Straight.

Two slightly different Teardrop designs were offered, the first called "Jeancourt" after the car's first buyer; and the second "New York" as it was first shown in the USA in 1937. Eleven "New York" cars were built on the T150 chassis and five "Jeancourt" cars were built — but interestingly, just one of these was built on a shorter, T23, chassis.

That car is unique. Not only does it display all the artistry and flair of the pre-war French coachbuilders, but it is also the only example built on the race-bred T23 chassis. When it came up for auction in October 2010 it was estimated to fetch between £1,100,000 and £1,400,000. In the event the hammer came down at an impressive £1,792,000.

Country of Origin:	France
Body Design:	Figoni & Falaschi
Manufacture Date:	1937-39
Power:	115bhp (85.7kW) @ 4100rpm
Maximum Torque:	n.a.
Top Speed:	115mph (185km/h)
0-60mph (0-97km/h):	11.5 secs
Transmission:	Wilson 4-speed pre-selector gearbox
Engine:	3,996cc straight six
Length:	4526mm (178 in.)
Width:	1790mm (70.5 in.)
Wheelbase:	2641mm (104 in.)
Kerb Weight:	1504kg (3,316 lbs.)
Brakes:	Drums
Suspension:	Independent with transverse leaf spring and friction dampers (F); Live rear axle with semi-elliptic leaf springs and friction dampers (R)
Auction Sale:	2010 £1,792,000 (€2,102,547; $2,762,874)

1939 MERCEDES-BENZ W154

For 1934, a new formula for Grand Prix racing was introduced with a maximum weight of 750kg so Mercedes-Benz and other competitors were forced to create a brand new racing car – and in the case of the Stuttgart firm, this was the W25.

With a stunning silver livery – legend has it that race manager Alfred Neubauer had the paint stripped off to save weight on the eve of the first race at the Nürburgring in June 1934 – the elegant W25 driven by Manfred von Brauchitsch won first time out and also set a new track record of 76mph (122.5km/h) in the process.

This turned out to be the first of many famous Silver Arrows victories which were continued with the W125 that was introduced in 1937. Then, for the new formula of 1938 Mercedes developed another revolutionary car – the V12, 3-litre W154. The new V12 was fitted with sophisticated cylinder heads with four valves per cylinder and a pair of Rootes-type superchargers at the front. Mercedes had toyed with the idea of introducing fuel injection on this model but in the end plumped for the more reliable carburettor technology. Unusually, the engine was canted over to one side to allow the prop shaft to be positioned alongside the driver.

Regulations that year allowed either a 4.5-litre naturally aspirated engine, or a 3.0-litre supercharged unit, and the Mercedes engineers determined that supercharging would result in a more competitive package.

They were proved right because the W154, which was even more successful than its predecessors, clocking up a string of victories on the world's racetracks and also, when fitted with a special streamlined body, recording the fastest speeds ever recorded on the open road: 268.75mph (432.7km/h) for the flying kilometre, and 268.57mph (432.4km/h) for the flying mile on the Frankfurt – Darmstadt autobahn.

The W154 absolutely dominated the 1938-39 season, winning 11 of the 16 races that were held before WW2 broke out in September. In total, just 15 W154s were built; many were destroyed during the war and of those that remain the vast majority are either owned by Mercedes-Benz or are already in museums.

One car still left in private hands had been stranded in Yugoslavia after von Brauchitsch had taken second place in the Belgrade Grand Prix just before war was declared. The car ended up in Romania where it was re-discovered in the late 1980s and subsequently restored.

The value of one of the world's greatest ever Grand Prix cars is estimated to be as high as £8,000,000.

Country of Origin:	Germany
Body Design:	Mercedes-Benz
Manufacture Date:	1938-39
Power:	476bhp (355kW) @ 7800rpm
Maximum Torque:	n.a.
Top Speed:	192mph (309km/h)
0-60mph (0-97km/h):	n.a.
Transmission:	5-speed manual
Engine:	2,961cc V12
Length:	4600mm (181 in.)
Width:	1850mm (72.8 in.)
Wheelbase:	2545mm (100.2 in.)
Kerb Weight:	980kg (2160 lbs.)
Brakes:	Hydraulic drums
Suspension:	Independent, with double wishbones, coil springs and hydraulic shock absorbers (F); De Dion axle with longitudinal torsion bars and hydraulic shock absorbers (R)
Estimated Value:	£8,000,000 (€9,386,371; $12,334,258)

1941 CHRYSLER THUNDERBOLT

Concept cars are such an integral part of the modern automobile industry that it's hard to imagine a time when they did not exist. But that was the situation in the 1930's until GM's visionary boss Harley Earl produced the revolutionary Buick Y-Job, a model that was never specifically designed for production but which offered a tantalising glimpse of what the future might hold.

Very quickly other manufacturers grasped the publicity potential of the concept car, and the Chrysler Thunderbolt was one of the earliest examples. Unveiled at the 1940 New York Auto Show alongside the radical but less futuristic Chrysler Newport, the Thunderbolt was designed by Alex Tremulis with a single flowing surface enclosing a standard C-26 chassis, Chrysler New Yorker running gear and the eight-cylinder engine from the C-27 Crown Imperial.

This full-envelope body was constructed almost entirely of aluminium — only the bonnet and boot lid were made of steel — and in the search for streamlining perfection the wheels were enclosed, the headlights were retractable and there was apparently no radiator grille. In fact, the air intakes were hidden below the front bumper.

Also unique was the world's first hardtop retractable roof which operated electrically at the touch of a button, sliding into the space behind the three-passenger front bench seat. Access to the luggage space was provided by a sliding lid mechanism. Equally as innovative was the push-button door release system and the hydraulically-operated window lifters.

No wonder that after the Thunderbolt's release in 1940 it created a massive stir right across the country as five differently-coloured examples were exhibited at Chrysler dealerships as part of a hectic promotional tour of what was billed "The Car of the Future".

The Thunderbolt took its name from George Eyston's land speed record-breaking car which was timed at Bonneville Salt Flats at 357.53mph (575.39 km/h) in 1938. Eyston's Thunderbolt was powered by a pair of 12-cylinder Rolls-Royce aero engines, though Chrysler's was a little more sedate: It had a 323.5 cubic-inch straight eight "Spitfire" engine that produced 143 horsepower and drove the rear wheels via a Chrysler Fluid Drive transmission. It was reported to have been capable of achieving over 100mph (160km/h).

Unusually for concept cars, after the nationwide dealer tour, the Chrysler Thunderbolts were sold to private buyers for around $6000 each. Four examples, including the one on display at the Walter P. Chrysler Museum in Detroit, are still known to survive. The last to be offered for sale in 2009 failed to reach its reserve despite a bid of $1,175,000. Its owner later offered it for sale at between $1,500,000 and $2,000,000.

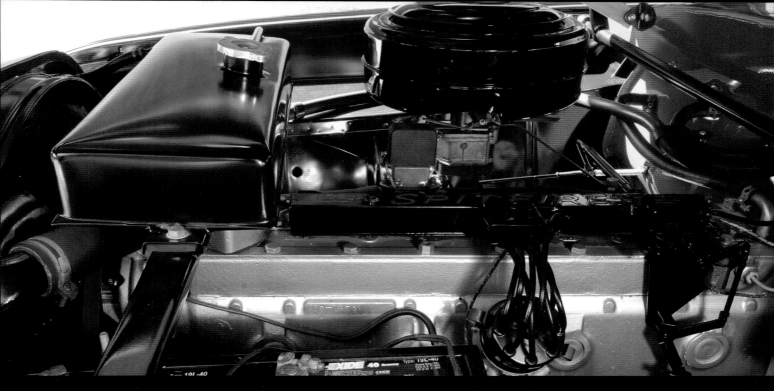

Country of Origin:	USA
Body Design:	Alex Tremulis
Manufacture Date:	1940-41
Power:	143bhp (107kW) @ 3400rpm
Maximum Torque:	270 lb.ft (366Nm) @ 1600rpm
Top Speed:	100mph (161km/h)
0-60mph (0-97km/h):	n.a.
Transmission:	3-speed Fluid Drive
Engine:	323.5 cu. in (5,301cc) straight eight
Length:	3990mm (157 in.)
Width:	1640mm (65 in.)
Wheelbase:	2440mm (145.5 in.)
Kerb Weight:	n.a.
Brakes:	Drums
Suspension:	Independent (F); Solid axle (R)
Estimated Value:	£970,000–1.3 million (€1.1–1.5 million; $1.5-2 million)

1948 FERRARI 166 SCAGLIETTI SPYDER

Enzo Ferrari built the first cars carrying his name in 1947, all destined for the race track and in that first busy season his cars competed in 14 events. With the season ended, Ferrari started to concentrate on a batch of just seven Tipo 166 2-litre Spyder Corsa cars that could be sold to customers. The "166" name derived from the cubic capacity of each of the engine's 12 cylinders. Five were built on a long wheelbase and just two were built on a shorter chassis. These may have been customer cars, but they remained out-and-out racers, being described at the time as "the most advanced unsupercharged sports car in the world today".

A typical example is what today is the supremely elegant Ferrari 166 Scaglietti Spyder. Back in 1948, when it emerged from the Ferrari factory gates in Maranello in northern Italy, it was just the seventh Spyder Corsa that Ferrari built and it sported a cycle-winged body by Ansaloni on a SWB chassis. Under the bonnet was a Gioacchino Colombo-designed 2-litre V12 with three Weber carburettors which could be tuned for up to 140bhp. Although destined for the public road, it was very much a racer and it was entered into the 1948 Bari Grand Prix with Giuseppe Farina behind the wheel.

For the next few seasons the 166 Spyder Corsa competed around Europe before it was sold to a private buyer who chose to commission new coachwork – something that was by no means unusual in those days. The coachbuilder was Sergio Scaglietti and not only was this one of the first bodies he had created for a Ferrari, but it was also one of his most elegant.

It was a full width sports body incorporating distinctive air outlets on each of the long, curved front wings. Not only is the body perfectly proportioned, but also supremely elegant and flowing.

But just as important is what is underneath the bodywork because although the very first 125 Ferrari was fitted a 1.5-litre engine, it was the slightly later Tipo 166 models with its 2-litre powerplant that created Ferrari's reputation, winning both the Mille Miglia and Targa Florio. It's no exaggeration to say that the Ferrari 166 was the start of a legend in the fields of motorsport and performance road cars.

This Scaglietti Spyder was exported to California in the mid-1950's and sold in 1969 for $4,000. The next time it came up for sale was 32 years later, when it was sold for more than a million dollars.

Country of Origin:	Italy
Body Design:	Scaglietti
Manufacture Date:	1949
Power:	140bhp (104kW) @ 6600rpm
Maximum Torque:	281 lb.ft (381Nm) @ 5500rpm
Top Speed:	135mph (217km/h)
0-60mph (0-97km/h):	n.a.
Transmission:	5-speed manual
Engine:	1,995cc V12
Length:	3658mm (144 in.)
Width:	1549mm (61 in.)
Wheelbase:	2229mm (90.5 in.)
Kerb Weight:	650kg (1433 lbs.)
Brakes:	Hydraulic drums
Suspension:	Double wishbones, transverse semi-elliptic leaf spring, friction dampers (F); Live axle with semi-elliptic leaf springs, Houdaille shock absorbers and trailing arms (R)
Auction Sale:	2007 £677,787 (€795,245; $1,045,000)

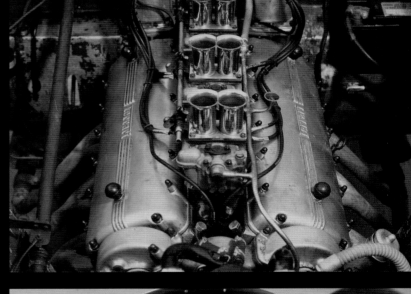

1948 TUCKER SEDAN

Preston Thomas Tucker was a man who at various times had worked in Cadillac's post-room, served as a police officer, was a Dodge and Studebaker car salesman and had perfected a gun turret during WW2 which provided him with a small fortune.

He chose to use that fortune to challenge the might of the Detroit Big Three — GM, Ford and Chrysler — with a large six-seater saloon featuring some extremely advanced technology.

Tucker at first planned to build a Tucker Torpedo sports car but later concentrated on the Tucker Sedan, a design that was in many ways far ahead of its time.

The original plan was for a large but lightweight aluminium 9,651cc flat-six engine designed for use in Bell helicopters but in fact a smaller 5,494cc unit built by Air Cooled Motors was fitted instead. It was converted to water cooling and mounted transversely at the rear driving a semi-automatic pre-selector transmission based upon a Cord design. In due course, it was planned to introduce a "Tuckermatic" full auto transmission.

Other novelties included a central headlamp that turned with the steering mechanism, disc brakes all round (later changed to drums) and some of the earliest passive safety measures — a padded dashboard, a split windscreen designed to pop out in an accident and even seat belts — though they were removed as it was felt that fitting belts implied the car was unsafe!

The imposing bodywork was the design of Alex Tremulis who had worked for Cord, Duesenberg and Auburn in the past. It looked stunning and performed well and on its launch in 1948 Tucker described his Sedan as "the first all-new car in 50 years".

Sadly, it failed to live up to its promises as Tucker was arrested and charged with fraud and other financial crimes (it was rumoured that Detroit's Big Three were behind the accusations though this was never proved). Tucker was eventually acquitted but the damage had been done and confidence in the product and the company plummeted. By the time receivers were called in, just 51 cars had been built at the massive former Dodge aircraft factory in Chicago that Tucker had leased.

Tucker later tried to build a new car company in Brazil but died of lung cancer before his efforts bore fruit. Today, the Tucker Sedan is such a rare and interesting sideline in the USA's automotive history that it's perhaps no wonder that the few remaining examples now command such high prices. Tucker tried to sell his Sedan for $2,450 in 1948. Today's' auction values are over a million dollars.

Country of Origin:	USA	Length:	5560mm (219 in.)
Body Design:	Alex Tremulis	Width:	2007mm (79 in.)
Manufacture Date:	1948	Wheelbase:	3250mm (128 in.)
Power:	166bhp (124kW) @ 3200rpm	Kerb Weight:	1600kg (3527 lbs.)
Maximum Torque:	372 lb.ft. (504Nm)	Brakes:	Drums
Top Speed:	118mph (190km/h)	Suspension:	Independent, rubber sandwich (F); Independent rubber sandwich (R)
0-60mph (0-97km/h):	10 secs		
Transmission:	4-speed pre-selector	Auction Sale:	2008 £659,951
Engine:	5,494cc flat six		(€ 774,318; $1,017,500)

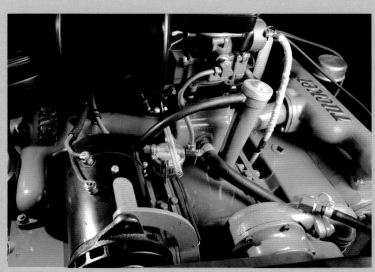

1952 JAGUAR C-TYPE

The Jaguar XK120 was launched in 1948, the company's first all-new post-war sports car. It was demonstrated on a closed section of Belgian motorway near Jabbeke at 132mph (213km/h), which was quick for its time and the car soon showed its promise at the 24 Hours of Le Mans race.

As a result, in 1951 Jaguar developed its first purpose-built racing car, the XK120C, with the "C" standing for "Competition". It used the engine and transmission of the standard XK120 but its construction was unique: it had a lightweight spaceframe chassis upon which an equally lightweight and highly aerodynamic aluminium body was mounted.

The smooth and purposeful body was the work of aviation aerodynamicist Malcolm Sayer. It was a no-nonsense design with no passenger door (and only a token passenger seat on top of the tool kit), no trunk and a front end design that allowed the whole nose section to be lifted on forward-mounted hinges to allow good access to the engine.

Initially, the C-Type's 3.4-litre 6-cylinder twin-cam engine produced 205bhp (153kW), which was substantially more than the standard road car which was tuned to between 160bhp (119kW) and 180bhp (134kW). Later, the C-Type was developed to produce more power thanks to triple Weber carburettors and higher-lift camshafts. Disc brakes replaced the earlier drum units and even more weight was saved by using a rubber fuel tank and lighter electrical components.

Three cars were entered into the Le Mans 24-hour race of 1951 and it won first time out at the hands of Peter Walker and Peter Whitehead. The other two cars, one of which was driven by Stirling Moss, retired, but the new car — by now known as the C-Type Jaguar, had certainly made its mark.

The C-Type won again at Le Mans in 1953 when Duncan Hamilton and Tony Rolt won at an average speed of 106mph (171km/h), the first time the race had been won at an average of over 100mph (161km/h). Before these wins, Jaguar was hardly known outside the UK; Le Mans provided it with worldwide positive publicity.

Only 52 C-Type Jaguars were ever built so it remains a genuine rarity. Many replicas have been produced (some of which are so good that they fetch good money in themselves), but on the very rare occasions when a genuine C-Type comes up for auction, prices are high, with a recent example going under the hammer at $2,530,000 in 2009. The car pictured here was once owned by Juan Manuel Fangio, so its value could be as high as $3,500,000.

Country of Origin:	UK
Body Design:	Malcolm Sayer
Manufacture Date:	1951-1952
Power:	200bhp (149kW) @ 5800rpm
Maximum Torque:	220 lb.ft (298Nm) @ 3900rpm
Top Speed:	150mph (241km/h)
0-60mph (0-97km/h):	8.1 secs
Transmission:	4-speed manual
Engine:	3,442cc straight six
Length:	3990mm (157 in.)
Width:	1640mm (65 in.)
Wheelbase:	2440mm (96 in.)
Kerb Weight:	939kg (2065 lbs.)
Brakes:	Drums
Suspension:	Independent wishbones, torsion bars (F); Live axle, trailing links, transverse torsion bar, Panhard rod (R)
Estimated Value:	£2,270,100 (€2,663,500; $3,500,000)

1953 FERRARI 250 MM SPYDER

The Ferrari 250 S was a one-off design built specifically to enter the 1952 Mille Miglia. It was constructed on a ladder frame created from large diameter oval-shaped steel tubing and was powered by the very latest version of Gioachino Colombo's wonderful V12 engine — the 3-litre unit that meant each of its 12 cylinders was of 250cc displacement, and hence the "250" name.

Amazingly, Colombo's V12 had originally been designed five years earlier as a 1.5-litre unit so by now it had doubled in displacement. The final increase in size had been achieved by increasing the bore to 73mm, and this created the ultimate derivative of the Colombo V12, big enough to market road cars and big enough to produce the sort of results on the world's racetracks that were to constantly bolster Ferrari's reputation.

After the 250 S driven by Giovanni Bracco duly won that year's Mille Miglia, Ferrari quickly developed a production car which was dubbed MM in honour of the Mille Miglia victory, but which was actually built on a different chassis even though it shared the 3-litre V12 engine.

The Ferrari 250 MM was significant because it was the first of a long and honourable line of Ferrari 250 production models than stretched from 1952 to 1963. Its wheelbase was increased from 2250mm to 2400mm and the power of its V12 was boosted from 230bhp to 240bhp thanks to the adoption of quad-choke Weber carburettors.

In all, just 31 Ferrari 250 MM models were built in the following year, 18 of which had a Berlinetta body sculpted by Pininfarina, while the remaining 13 were fitted with bodies by Vignale. 12 of these were Spyders in three distinct series, while just one Vignale-bodied coupe was made.

In truth, the 250 MM wasn't particularly successful at the major international events as it was soon overshadowed by the faster 340 MM, but entered by privateers on both sides of the Atlantic, it clocked up plenty of victories in GT racing.

But what makes the 250 MM truly significant is that it led directly on to the Ferrari 250 GT which was launched in 1954 — and that combination of "250" and "GT" is about as significant as it gets in the history of automotive supercars.

Every Ferrari 250 MM is important but chassis 0348MM was originally sold to Alfred Momo. He was technician to Briggs Cunningham who had the distinction of racing and winning in the very first Ferrari imported to the USA. That car came up for auction twice in 2004, making $1,500,000 in August and then $1,650,000 just a month later.

Country of Origin:	Italy
Body Design:	Vignale
Manufacture Date:	1952-1953
Power:	240bhp (179kW) @ 7200rpm
Maximum Torque:	n.a.
Top Speed:	137mph (220km/h)
0-60mph (0-97km/h):	5.1 secs.
Transmission:	4-speed manual
Engine:	2,953cc V12
Length:	4390mm (172.8 in.)
Width:	1650mm (65 in.)
Wheelbase:	2600mm (102.4 in.)
Kerb Weight:	1065kg (2350 lbs.)
Brakes:	Drums
Suspension:	Double wishbones, single transverse leaf spring (F); Live axle, semi-elliptical longitudinal leaf springs (R)
Auction Sale:	2004 £1,650,000 (€1,935,939; $2,543,941)

1953 FERRARI 375 MM SPYDER 340 HP

Aurelio Lampredi was an engineering genius, employed by Enzo Ferrari to produce a new V12 for his F1 cars in 1951 after Ferrari had been comprehensively beaten by Alfa Romeo to the very first Formula One Championship in 1950.

Lampredi produced a new 4.5-litre naturally aspirated V12 with lightweight alloy cylinder heads and block which produced some 350bhp – more than enough to be competitive. In fact, Alfa Romeo withdrew from F1 at the end of the 1951 season, and with Ferrari the only competitive team left, the FIA decided that for the next two years the F1 Championship would be run under F2 regulations.

On the face of it, the new Lampredi V12 was redundant but Ferrari had other ideas and quickly sketched out ideas for a lightweight two-seater body to be powered by the F1 engine for competition in GT races. The very first cars were fitted with exactly the same engine as the previous season's F1 cars had used but to improve reliability, later cars had the bore increased and the stroke reduced to allow for higher-revving performance.

The car was called the Ferrari 375 MM, and in the next two years 26 were built with the majority being fitted with Pininfarina Spyder bodies though a few had Pininfarina Berlinetta bodies and five were fitted with custom bodies by independent coachbuilders.

The car was an immediate success around the world, though it sadly failed to win at Le Mans in 1954, mainly because its antiquated drum brakes were no match for the disc brakes on the rival Jaguar C-Type. However, a revised version, the 375 Plus fitted with a larger 4,954cc engine, did win the prestigious event in 1954.

The Ferrari 375 MM pictured started life in 1953 as a Pininfarina Spyder but in 1954 it was returned to Ferrari for a unique new body crafted by Scaglietti. Scaglietti, of course, would later develop a far closer relationship with Ferrari and was destined to become the coachbuilder Ferrari turned to first for the majority of its competition cars. This body – chassis number 0366AM – is especially interesting because it's an earlier pointer to later classic Ferrari designs, including the legendary 250 Testa Rossa.

When offered for sale in 2005, it failed to sell despite a top bid of $2,225,000, its owner understandably perhaps believing it was worth considerably more.

Country of Origin:	Italy
Body Design:	Scaglietti
Manufacture Date:	1953-54
Power:	340bhp (253.5kW) @ 7000rpm
Maximum Torque:	n.a.
Top Speed:	n.a.
0-60mph (0-97km/h):	n.a.
Transmission:	4-speed manual
Engine:	4,522cc V12
Length:	4175mm (164.4 in.)
Width:	1325mm (52.2 in.)
Wheelbase:	2600mm (102.3 in.)
Kerb Weight:	1090kg (2400 lbs.)
Brakes:	Drums
Suspension:	Parallel unequal length A arms with transverse leaf spring, sway bar and lever dampers (F); Live axle, semi-elliptic leaf springs, parallel arms, lever dampers (R)
Estimated Value:	2005 More than £1,443,135 (€1,693,225; $2,225,000)

1953 MASERATI A6 GCS

It was not unusual in the 1950s for manufacturers to produce sports cars that were loosely based on their track racing cars and one of the most successful was the Maserati A6 GCS, which was powered by Maserati's Formula 2 DOHC short stroke 2-litre engine. For the road racer, engineer Gioachino Colombo — who had recently moved from Ferrari to Maserati — designed a ladder-frame chassis manufactured from oval-shaped steel tubing onto which an elegant, curvaceous Spyder body by Fantuzzi was fitted. Between 1953 and 1955, a total of 53 Maserati A6 GCS cars were built, all with Fantuzzi Spyder bodywork except for four Pininfarina-bodied coupés and one each Frua and Vignale Spyders.

The twin-overhead cam 2-litre straight six engine with its aluminium block was unusual in that it featured two spark plugs per cylinder and revved freely to 7300rpm and produced 170bhp, so performance was sparkling for the day, helped by Colombo's efforts to equalise weight distribution by locating the gearbox with the rear transaxle.

The suspension design also owed much to that of the Formula 2 car, with double wishbones at the front and transverse leaf springs at the rear. Braking was via Dunlop discs and unsprung weight was kept to a minimum thanks to Borrani wire wheels.

The new car soon showed its potential, winning many races around the world including class wins and fifth overall for Giletti and Berttocchi in the 1953 Mille Miglia and impressive showings in the Targa Florio and Pescara events.

Maserati A6 GCS chassis number 2053 was originally sold in the USA to P. Ducati Motors and is believed to have been driven by Juan Manuel Fangio at the Thompson Raceway in October 1953. Later a Chevrolet V8 was fitted and later still it was used as a street car. It was restored after being sold in 1989 and restored again in 1998 to return it to its original condition and specification. This included fitting a reproduction of the original Maserati engine. However, when offered for sale in late 2010, an original engine number 2067 was part of the deal, and could be fitted by a subsequent owner should he or she wish. Interestingly, that original and genuine engine was rated at 202bhp, considerably more than the figure of 170bhp quoted back in 1953 when the car was introduced.

The faithful restoration has returned the cabin to its sparse, silver painted original, with its bright teal gauges intended to be easily read at speed. Its asking price in 2010 was $1,850,000.

PARKING FOR THE
59th St. GROUP
ONLY
Violators will be cited
and or towed at
Vehicle owner's expense
22950-A C.V.C.
For towed vehicles call
Emeryville Police Dept.
596-3700

Country of Origin:	Italy
Body Design:	Fantuzzi
Manufacture Date:	1953-1954
Power:	170bhp (126.7kW) @ 7300rpm
Maximum Torque:	NA
Top Speed:	147mph (235km/h)
0-60mph (0-97km/h):	n.a.
Transmission:	5-speed manual
Engine:	1,986cc six-cylinder
Length:	3840mm (151.2 in.)
Width:	1530mm (60.2 in.)
Wheelbase:	2310mm (90.0 in.)
Kerb Weight:	740kg (1628 lbs.)
Brakes:	Drums front and rear
Suspension:	Independent with coil springs, anti-roll bar and Houdaille hydraulic shock absorbers (F); Rigid axle with longitudinal leaf springs, anti-roll bar and Houdaille hydraulic shock absorbers (R)
Estimated Value:	2010 £1,199,910 (€1,407,850; $1,850,000)

1954 FERRARI 250 MONZA SPYDER

During the early 1950's Ferrari produced a bewildering number of new models, making use of his available engines to create cars both for his works racing team and for wealthy customers to race themselves.

Thus for 1954, the 500 Mondial used a 2-litre in-line four-cylinder engine, while the 750 Monza had a 3-litre four-cylinder engine. Then, that same year, Ferrari decided a more powerful competitor was required so he fitted the Colombo V12 that had already proved itself in the 250 MM into a slightly lengthened 750 Monza ladder-type chassis to create the Ferrari 250 Monza. It shared the 750 Monza's independent suspension and recently-introduced De Dion rear axle.

The V12 was very similar to that in the 250 MM but in the 250 Monza, each of the 12 cylinders had its own individual intake port in place of the earlier Siamese design. The new heads, when fitted with three four-barrel Weber carburettors, produced a healthy 240bhp.

Just four of these 250 Monzas were made, two of them having a Pininfarina Berlinetta body similar to the 500 Mondials, and the other two being clothed in a Scaglietti Spyder body that was very similar to the 750 Monza's. Scaglietti may have constructed the aluminium body, but it is reported that the design was actually the work of young Dino Ferrari, Enzo's son.

Ferrari retained the first 250 Monza for the works competition team and the other three were sold to customers in Italy who raced them with some success.

The car's first competitive outing was at the Monza Autodromo in June 1954, from which the car gets its name. Later in 1954 it was entered into the gruelling Carrera Panamericana Mexico, the last year this famous 2,000-mile race would be held. The 250 Monza came fifth overall, a creditable result against far more powerful opposition from Ferrari 375 Plus and 375 MM cars.

Of the four original Ferrari 250 Monza cars, one of the two Pininfarina Spyders was re-bodied in 1957 by Ferrari's USA importer Luigi Chinetti, who commissioned Scaglietti to produce a new Spyder in the style of the 250 TR.

One of the two Scaglietti Spyders, Spyder chassis 0442M which had competed at the Carrera Panamericana and which is believed to be the only one of the four 250 Monza cars to have retained its original bodywork was sold at auction in 2002 for $1,705,000 though it is reported that later it was displayed at the 2007 Retromobile in Paris where it was sold and later offered for sale again at a price of some £5.5 million.

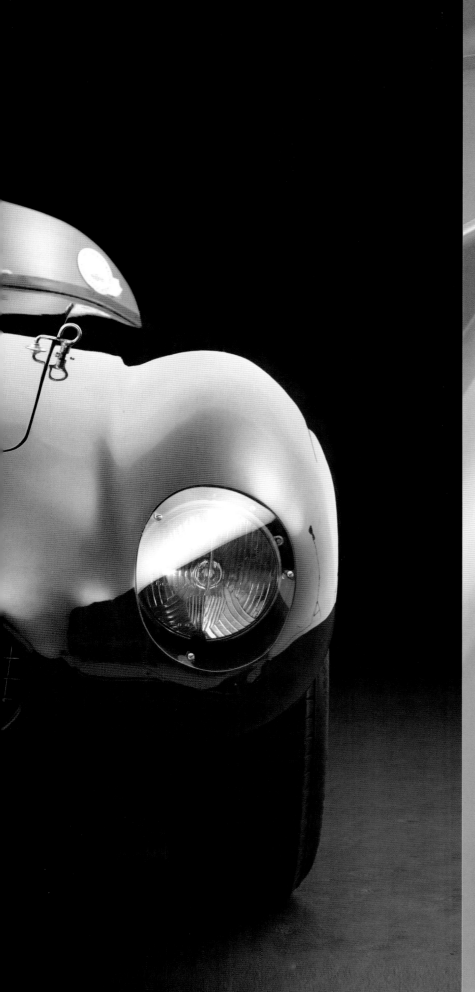

Country of Origin:	Italy
Body Design:	Scaglietti
Manufacture Date:	1953-54
Power:	240bhp (179kW) @ 7200rpm
Maximum Torque:	n.a.
Top Speed:	n.a.
0-60mph (0-97km/h):	n.a.
Transmission:	4-speed manual
Engine:	2,953cc V12
Length:	4175mm (164.4 in.)
Width:	1325mm (52.2 in.)
Wheelbase:	2250mm (88.6 in.)
Kerb Weight:	850kg (1870 lbs.)
Brakes:	Drums
Suspension:	Parallel unequal length A arms with transverse leaf spring, coil springs and dampers (F); De Dion axle, transverse leaf spring, and dampers (R)
Estimated Value:	2007 £5,500,000 (€6,453,130; $8,479,803)

1955 JAGUAR D-TYPE 3.4 LITRE SPORTS

The Jaguar D-Type was developed with a single purpose in mind: to follow up the C-Type's wins at Le Mans in 1951 and 1953 with yet another victory. It shared the earlier C-Type's six-cylinder XK engine but that was as far as the similarities went: the D-Type had a bespoke monocoque chassis welded to a sub-frame and a highly aerodynamic body featuring a distinctive vertical fin at the rear intended to maintain stability at high speeds on the long Mulsanne Straight at Le Mans.

The engine was uprated to 240bhp with dry-sump lubrication being specified to reduce oil surge during cornering and also to reduce the height of the engine so a more aerodynamic profile could be designed.

Magnesium alloy was employed on the early cars for the framework, body and suspension parts. This resulted in reduced weight but it was massively expensive both to manufacture and repair so for 1955 aluminium and steel was employed instead.

The D-Type enjoyed an encouraging debut, with Duncan Hamilton and Tony Rolt coming second in the 1954 24 Hours of Le Mans. Then the following year a longer nose was fitted to boost the top speed and improve the airflow over the front of the car and the D-Type driven by Mike Hawthorn and Ivor Bueb duly won at Le Mans in 1955 — a race that is mainly remembered for Pierre Levegh's Mercedes-Benz SLR being launched into the crowd following an on-course accident that resulted in 80 deaths.

Mercedes withdrew from racing at the end of that season, but undeterred, the Jaguar Ecurie Ecosse team went on to win at Le Mans again in both 1956 and 1957. In total, Jaguar built 68 D-Types though only 43 of them raced. Jaguar then planned to convert the remaining 25 to make them street-legal. Bumpers, more instrumentation, a passenger seat and a passenger door were fitted and the fin was removed to create the Jaguar XKSS. In the event, only 16 were converted before a factory fire brought work on the project to a halt.

The D-Type was Jaguar's most successful racing car and with relatively few D-Types being built, values are inevitably high, especially for cars with a racing or a celebrity owner pedigree. A D-Type raised $4,400,00 in 2008 which set a new world record price for one of these iconic cars. Since then, D-Types that have appeared at auction have not reached quite that heady level, though in early 2010 the hammer fell on another D-Type at $3,740,000.

Country of Origin:	UK
Body Design:	Malcolm Sayer
Manufacture Date:	1954-56
Power:	245bhp (183kW) @ 6000rpm
Maximum Torque:	240 lb.ft (325Nm) @ 4000rpm
Top Speed:	170mph (274km/h)
0-60mph (0-97km/h):	7.0 secs
Transmission:	4-speed manual
Engine:	3,442cc straight six
Length:	3912mm (154 in.)
Width:	1664mm (65.5 in.)
Wheelbase:	2300mm (90.6 in.)
Kerb Weight:	840kg (1852 lbs.)
Brakes:	Disc
Suspension:	Double wishbones, torsion bars, telescopic dampers (F); Solid axle with trailing links, transverse torsion bar, telescopic dampers (R).
Auction Sale:	January 2010 £2,425,764 (€2,846,140; $3,740,000)

1955 MERCEDES-BENZ 300 SLS PROTOTYPE ROADSTER

Unique is a word that's often misused, but just occasionally it can justifiably be used to describe a car. This one, chassis number 00009/52, started life in 1952 as a Mercedes-Benz SL Gullwing Coupé, built by the Mercedes Racing Department to compete at Le Mans. Driven by Helfrich and Niedermayoer it duly came second to another Mercedes SL, then went on to come third at the Nürburgring Sports Car Championship and to run strongly in the Mexican Carrera Panamericana before being disqualified on a technicality.

After that, the car was used for various testing purposes, first being fitted with a new fuel injected engine in 1953 and the following year being used as a running prototype for the proposed new 300SL Roadster.

During the course of 1955, the car's chassis was modified to increase stiffness (essential to prevent excessive scuttleshake since torsional stiffness is inevitably lost in removing the roof structure) and a new roadster body designed by Freidrich Geiger was fitted. At this time, the car was registered as a road car in Germany and testing continued until the end of 1956, at which time the car, now designated the "300 SLS" (for Super Light Special), was revealed to the press in the company of Sports Car Club of America (SCCA) Champion Paul O'Shea.

O'Shea then showed at the Nürburgring and other circuits that the new 300 SLS had serious motorsport potential and Mercedes decided to build two more 300 SLS cars specifically to compete in the SCCA series in 1957. Paul O'Shea in one of the new racing 300SLS won the Class D SCCA Championship, while the original prototype continued to be used for testing purposes by Mercedes-Benz, including in the development of a new removable hard top for the 300SL Roadster – the soft-top car that was launched in 1957 at the Geneva Motor Show, based on the original 300 SLS Prototype.

According to factory records the 300 SLS Prototype remained at Mercedes-Benz until 1965 when it was sold to a private owner. It passed through a number of owners' hands before arriving in California in 1987 where Scott Grunfor started a full restoration. It was then sold to a Japanese collector, but returned to Pebble Beach for the Concours event in both 1991 and 1997.

The Mercedes 300 SLS Prototype is a unique car and so difficult to value but it's confidently estimated that were it to be offered for sale, it's unlikely that the hammer would fall until a bid of at least $1,500,000 had been made.

Country of Origin:	Germany
Body Design:	Mercedes-Benz
Manufacture Date:	1955
Power:	240bhp (179kW) @ 5800rpm
Maximum Torque:	309Nm (228 lb.ft.) @ 5000rpm
Top Speed:	165mph (265km/h)
0-60mph (0-97km/h):	7.2 secs
Transmission:	4-speed manual
Engine:	2,996cc straight six
Length:	4520mm (178 in.)
Width:	1790mm (70.5 in.)
Wheelbase:	2400mm (94.5 in.)
Kerb Weight:	1093kg (2351bs.)
Brakes:	Front discs, rear drums;
Suspension:	Double wishbones, coil springs, stabiliser bar (F); High pivot swing axle, radius arms and coil springs (R)
Estimated Value:	£ 972,900 (€1,141,500; $1,500,000)

1956 MASERATI TIPO 52 200SI SPORT INTERNAZIONALE

Maserati's 1.5-litre 150S sports car was successful from its first appearance at the 1955 Nürburgring 500km race when Jean Behra qualified in pole position and went on to dominate the race until the chequered flag. After that the pretty little two-seater, which looked like a scaled down version of the mighty Maserati 300S, continued to dominate despite opposition from the likes of Lotus, Porsche and Cooper.

As a result, Maserati's next step was to bore the engine out to 2-litres, and fit bigger valves and larger Weber carburettors to boost the power output from 140bhp to 186bhp. Under the skin, the chassis was virtually identical to that of the 150S while the bodywork was again a re-working of the 300S's lines and proportions.

From 1955 to 1957 Maserati offered the 200S to wealthy private customers who wanted to race, while also running a factory team. Maserati's 200S was driven by Franco Bordoni at the 1955 Imola Grand Prix but it failed to impress either there, or at the Targa Florio later that season.

In 1957 the 200S became the 200SI — standing for Sport Internazionale — which meant the car adhered to the latest racing regulations. By this time the original 200S had been developed to improve its handling with the adoption of a De Dion rear axle and improved braking. Maserati had built four rigid axle examples but the later cars were built on a tubular chassis constructed by Gilco before returning to the Maserati works for modifications. In addition, the longer nosed body was the work of Merdardo Fantuzzi who took over responsibility for the bodywork from Celestino Fiandri who had built the first few bodies.

The Maserati 200SI was more successful in the 1956 and 1957 seasons, at the end of which production ceased, and the car's last competitive appearance was at the Sicily Grand Prix of 1957 which was won by Scarlatti. With 32 examples sold, the 200SI was certainly a commercial success for Maserati though it was a long way from being one of the company's most successful racers, perhaps because its tricky handing could only truly be mastered by professional racing drivers rather than wealthy amateurs.

The very first 200SI, a Maserati factory car with chassis number 2401 was raced by Jean Behra in the 1957 Venezuelan Grand Prix, winning the 2-litre class. Subsequent owners participated in numerous Concours and Historic Racing events, and when this very well-known Maserati came up for auction in 2010 it achieved a well-deserved $2,640,000 price tag.

Country of Origin:	Italy
Body Design:	Fantuzzi
Manufacture Date:	1955-57
Power:	190bhp (140kW) @ 7,500rpm
Maximum Torque:	n.a.
Top Speed:	162mph (261km/h)
0-60mph (0-97km/h):	n.a.
Transmission:	4 or 5-speed manual
Engine:	1,994cc straight four
Length:	3900mm (153.5 in.)
Width:	1450mm (57 in.)
Wheelbase:	2250mm (86.6 in.)
Kerb Weight:	670kg (1,477 lbs.).
Brakes:	Hydraulic drums
Suspension:	Independent with coil springs, torsion bar and shock absorbers (F); De Dion axle with transverse leaf spring with shock absorbers (R)
Price at Auction:	2010 £1,712,304 (€2,009,040; $2,640,000)

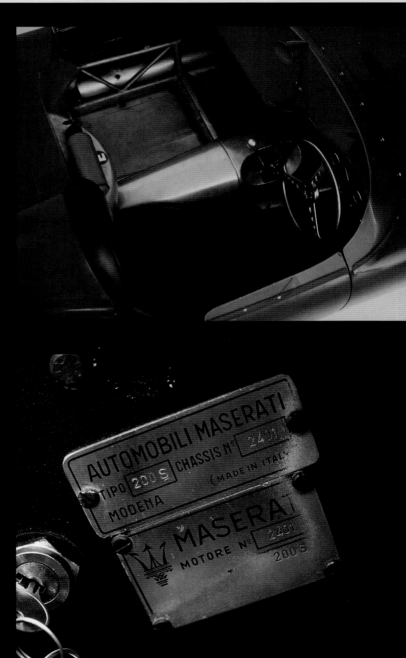

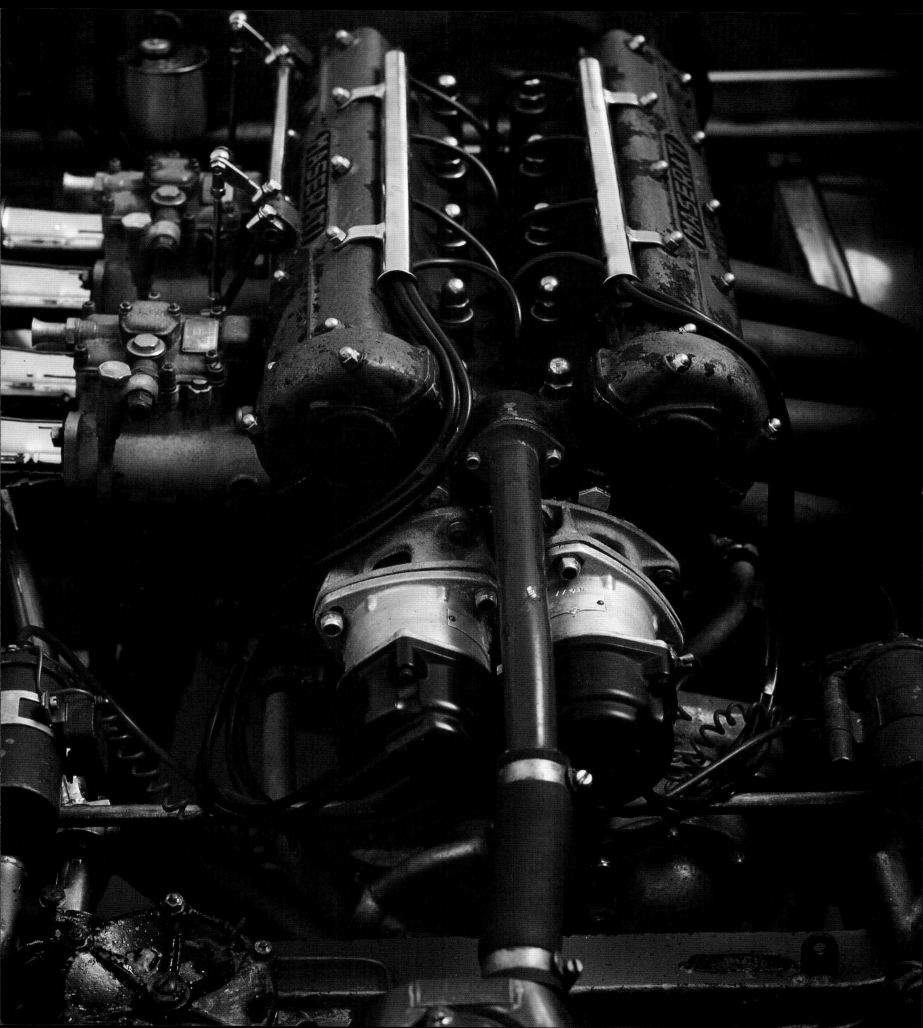

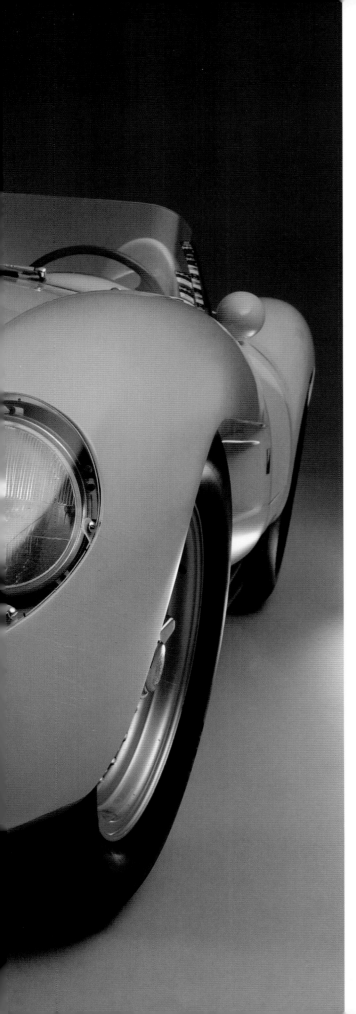

1957 FERRARI 250 PONTOON FENDER TESTA ROSSA

In 2009 a black Pontoon Fender 1957 Ferrari 250 Testa Rossa went under the hammer at $12.4 million. The following year, in 2010, another example, this time a 1958 model sporting a yellow and green livery, went unsold at auction despite a top bid of over $10 million.

What is it that makes this Ferrari so special?

It's partly because every one that was built has an even chassis number, which tells the Ferraristi that they were built for racing. It was driven by all the greats of that era — including Jean Behra, Pedro Rodriguez, Wolfgang Von Trips, Phil Hill, Dan Gurney, Carroll Shelby, Mike Hawthorn and Peter Collins. And its record is unsurpassed, with four Le Mans victories and four World Constructor's Championships thanks to taking the chequered flag at 10 of the 19 Championship races between 1958 and 1961. No wonder that Designer Sergio Scaglietti famously described the 250 Testa Rossa as a "Formula 1 cars with fenders."

It's also partly because only 21 of the distinctive Pontoon Fender Testa Rossas were built, making them even rarer than the other classic Ferrari of that time, the 250 GTO.

But mainly it's because, alongside a stunning racing pedigree and a high degree of rarity, the Ferrari 250 Testa Rossa is quite simply one of the most beautiful cars ever conceived. The flowing body work by Sergio Scaglietti is dramatic and aggressive and at the same time elegant and stylish. It's truly Italian automotive design at its very finest.

Under the long curved bonnet is a 3-litre single overhead cam V12 which produced 300bhp (223kW) — and in tribute to the engineers who had achieved 100bhp per litre, the cam covers were painted red; hence the name Testa Rossa — Italian for "Red Head".

This provided stunning performance, with 0-100mph (0-161km/h) acceleration in only 16 seconds and a top speed of 167mph (269km/h). Of the 250 Testa Rossa's rivals on the track, the Maserati 450S was more powerful, the Aston Martin DBR1 had superior aerodynamics, while both the Aston and the Jaguar D-Type were fitted with the latest, far more effective disc brakes. And yet it was the Ferrari that won time and time again, proving that its brilliance as a whole package could overcome shortcomings in individual areas.

No wonder that the Ferrari 250 Testa Rossa remains one of the most desirable cars of all time — with stratospheric values to match.

Country of Origin:	Italy
Body Design:	Scaglietti
Manufacture Date:	1957-1958
Power:	300bhp (223kW) @ 7200rpm
Maximum Torque:	281 lb.ft (381Nm) @ 5500rpm
Top Speed:	167mph (269km/h)
0-60mph (0-97km/h):	6.0 secs
Transmission:	4-speed manual
Engine:	2,953cc V12
Length:	3959mm (156 in.)
Width: I	523mm (60 in.)
Wheelbase:	2250mm (89 in.)
Kerb Weight:	794kg (1746 lbs.)
Brakes:	Aluminium drums
Suspension:	Unequal A-arms with coil springs, Houdaille shock absorbers and anti-roll bar (F); Live axle with semi-elliptic leaf springs, Houdaille shock absorbers and trailing arms (R)
Auction Sale:	2009 £7,912,920 (€9,284,200; $12,200,000)

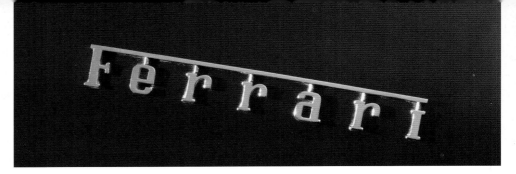

1958 FERRARI 250 GT CALIFORNIA SPYDER LWB

Enzo Ferrari created a completely new market in the 1950s when he launched the Gran Turismo or GT concept – essentially cars which were not out-and-out racers but which were designed primarily for road use. So, while Ferrari still produced Berlinettas for racing, it also started offering more comfortable coupés and elegant Pininfarina cabriolets.

The open-topped cabriolets were especially popular in the USA but the two Ferrari distributors there – Luigi Chinetti on the East Coast and John von Neumann on the West Coast – identified yet another market niche. They proposed a convertible version of the more powerful Berlinetta, and Ferrari quickly obliged, producing a prototype of the 250 GT California Spyder in 1957.

The Pininfarina-designed body, which was actually manufactured by Scaglietti, looked similar to the cabriolet, but with more aggressive styling, which was fitting as the engine was exactly the same as that fitted to the 250 GT "Tour de France" Berlinetta. The new Spyder also shared the 250 GT's tubular ladder chassis, suspension set up and 3-litre V12 engine.

The result was a new model that offered both supercar performance and extreme desirability. It was capable of reaching 145mph (233km/h) and was just as much at home on Santa Monica's boulevards as it was at the Laguna Seca raceway.

An initial run of 47 California Spyders were built, some of which were ordered with a lighter all-aluminium body and a more powerful engine by those wishing to go racing. From the outset the new car was a success on the racetrack, with Bob Grossman and Fernand Tavano taking fifth place at Le Mans in 1959 and Richie Ginther and Howard Hively taking an outright win at the Sebring 12-Hours race the same year.

The following year, 1960, a revised California Spyder was introduced with engine, braking and suspension modifications that improved the car's racing potential. At the same time the wheelbase was shortened in order to reduce weight still further and improve handing. In all, around 57 SWB California Spyders were sold, which means only a handful over 100 California Spyders were built by the time that production ended in February 1963.

Even though not many examples were built, the California Spyder worked wonders in opening the USA market to Ferrari. Because of its relative rarity but also because this is considered one of the most elegant cars Ferrari ever produced, values remain massively high, which is why the latest LWB California Spyder to come up for auction made more than $2,000,000.

Country of Origin:	Italy
Body Design:	Pininfarina
Manufacture Date:	1957-60
Power:	240bhp (179kW) @ 7000rpm
Maximum Torque:	188 lb.ft (255Nm) @ 5500rpm
Top Speed:	160mph (257km/h)
0-60mph (0-97km/h):	8.0 secs
Transmission:	4-speed manual
Engine:	2,953cc V12
Length:	4400mm (173.2 in.)
Width:	1650mm (65 in.)
Wheelbase:	2600mm (102.4 in.)
Kerb Weight:	1200kg (2640 lbs.)
Brakes:	Drums
Suspension:	Double wishbones, coil springs, telescopic dampers (F); Live axle, coil springs, telescopic dampers (R)
Auction Sale:	2010 £1,694,468 (€1,988,112 ;$2,612,500)

1959 FERRARI 250 GT TDF BERLINETTA

During the 1950s one of the most gruelling motorsport events — for both cars and drivers — was the Tour de France. It involved some 5,000km spread over five or six days of competition, taking in various circuit races, hill climbs and sprints mainly in France, but on occasions going over the borders into Belgium, Germany and Italy.

In 1956 Alphonso de Portago — a Spanish nobleman who competed in the 1956 Winter Olympics in Spain's bobsled team and was the French amateur jockey champion three times — entered the Tour de France in his Ferrari 250 GT Berlinetta and won. The following three years the event was won by Olivier Gendebien in another 250 GT Berlinetta, and as a result the car took on an unofficial name — the 250 GT Tour de France or TdF.

In all, 72 examples of the 250 GT TdF were built, though the cars were by no means all the same. The basic design revolved around the 250 GT competition car that was designed by Pininfarina and which was one of the highlights of the 1955 Paris Motor Show. Just a few months later, at the 1956 Geneva Motor Show, Scaglietti revealed its 250 GT Berlinetta which went into production later that year. All the early cars featured 14 louvres in the sail panel behind the cockpit, while later models had three louvres, and the last few cars built had just one. Just a few of the later cars had open headlights and five super-light cars with bodywork by Zagato were built.

The chassis remained relatively unchanged though the front suspension was adapted from transverse leaf springs to more effective coil springs. The gearbox also remained more or less unchanged though later cars had new synchromesh designed by Porsche installed. The engines were all Colombo-designed three-litre V12s though these were developed during the life of the 250 GT to boost power output.

The Ferrari 250 GT was the most successful 3-litre sports car of its generation, winning not only at the Tour de France but at all the world's major events, including the Mille Miglia, Targa Florio, Le Mans and the World Sports car Championships. It's one of the cars that truly has Ferrari's DNA coursing through its veins — a highly successful competition car that is also elegant, purposeful and beautiful to look at.

No wonder that when RM Auctions offered a 1959 250 GT TdF Berlinetta in London in 2008, its estimate was between £1,800,000 and £2,200,000 but bidding went even higher, with the hammer finally falling at £2,255,000.

Country of Origin:	Italy
Body Design:	Scaglietti
Manufacture Date:	1956-1959
Power:	250bhp (186.4kW) @ 7000rpm
Maximum Torque:	188 lb.ft (255Nm) @ 5500rpm
Top Speed:	n.a.
0-60mph (0-97km/h):	n.a.
Transmission:	4-speed manual
Engine:	2,953cc V12
Length:	4390mm (172.8 in.)
Width:	1650mm (65 in.)
Wheelbase:	2600mm (102.4 in.)
Kerb Weight:	1060kg (2337 lbs.)
Brakes:	Drums
Suspension:	Double wishbones, coil springs, lever-type dampers (F); Live axle, coil springs, lever-type dampers (R)
Auction Sale:	2008 £2,255,000 (€2,645,783; $3,476,719)

1959 FERRARI 246 S DINO

Enzo Ferrari's son Dino died of muscular dystrophy at the early age of 24 but before his untimely death in 1957 he had encouraged Vittorio Jano to create a new V6 engine for Ferrari. The engine was launched the following year, powering the Ferrari F1 cars to success in the F1 Championship and Mike Hawthorn to the Drivers' Championship, and became known thereafter as the 'Dino'.

It wasn't long before Ferrari fitted the Dino engine into sports cars, first a 2-litre derivative into the 196 S in 1958 and later the same year a 2.9-litre version, the 296 S. At this time a new naming system was introduced, with the first two numbers denoting the engine capacity and the third, the number of cylinders.

For the 1959 season, three more Dino cars were built, one fitted with a smaller engine and designated 196 S and the other two – which were run as Ferrari works racers – fitted with 2.4-litre derivatives and called the Ferrari 246 S Dino. Their V6 engines were relatively straightforward naturally aspirated units with double overhead camshafts operating two valves per cylinder. Fuel was fed through three Weber carburettors. These cars were also fitted with more advanced fully independent suspension systems, with double wishbones replacing the older live axle at the rear, which improved both handling and roadholding. The slippery, aerodynamic aluminium bodywork was by Fantuzzi and, although smaller with a shorter wheelbase, the cars looked so similar to the earlier V12 250 Testa Rossa that the easiest way to tell them apart was to look through the flexiglass engine cover and count the number of intake trumpets.

The cars managed to hold their own, and gained a second place in the 1960 Targa Florio but sports car design had be now moved on and mid-engined competitors were proving faster. Ferrari itself was to go down this route with the 246 SP of 1961, the company's first rear-engined sports car.

Of the two 246 S cars, chassis number 0778 suffered a major pit lane fire at the Nürburgring in 1960 which left much of its aluminium bodywork melted and its chassis exposed to the elements. However, it was rebuilt by Ferrari and sold to Luigi Chinetti's NART racing team in the USA where it was entered into the Sebring 12-Hours race driven by Jim Hall, who was later to come to fame with his Chaparral racing cars.

The car's engine was later changed for a 2-litre unit but was restored to its original specification in 2006. Its value today is believed to be at least $3,000,000.

Country of Origin:	Italy	Length:	n.a.
Body Design:	Fantuzzi	Width:	n.a.
Manufacture Date:	1959-60	Wheelbase:	2160mm (85 in.)
Power:	240bhp (179kW) @ 7500rpm	Kerb Weight:	680kg (1500 lbs.)
Maximum Torque:	n.a.	Brakes:	Discs
Top Speed:	n.a.	Suspension:	Double wishbones with coil springs
0-60mph (0-97km/h):	n.a.		and dampers (F); Double wishbones
Transmission:	5-speed manual		with coil springs and dampers (R)
Engine:	2,417cc V6	Private Treaty Sale:	2008 £1,945,800
			(€2,283,000 ;$3,000,000)

1960 ASTON MARTIN DB4 GT

The British company Aston Martin was bought by industrialist Sir David Brown in 1947 who provided hard cash both to develop a new road car and to support a racing team. The results were a brand new DB4 model that was unveiled at the 1958 London Motor Show and the victor's laurels at both Le Mans and the World Sports Car Championship in 1959.

The DB4 had an all-new 3,670cc straight six engine which produced 240bhp and provided a top speed of some 140mph (225km/h) together with acceleration from 0-60mph in around nine seconds. It had a pressed steel chassis upon which was mounted a lightweight (Superleggera) body by Touring of Milan, which was so in proportions that it stayed in production until 1970, being carried over, with minor amendments, to the subsequent DB5 and DB6 models. Thanks mainly to its sleek, elegant, powerful and sporting style, the DB4 was an immediate success and started the transformation of the company which over many years had enjoyed sporting success but whose road cars had failed to set the world alight.

Just a year after the launch of the DB4, following customer requests to Aston Martin for a lighter and more powerful derivative, the DB4 GT made its first appearance, driven by Stirling Moss at Silverstone where he took pole position, posted the fastest lap and took the chequered flag.

The performance transformation is explained by a reduction in the DB4 GT's length by 127mm (5 in.), slimmer aluminium panels than those fitted to the standard car and the use of plexiglass instead of glass in some of the windows. In all, 84kg (190 lbs.) was shaved off the weight. At the same time the engine was fitted with a twin-plug cylinder head, higher compression ratio, higher-lift camshafts and three twin-choke side-draft Weber carburettors tuned to produce 302bhp. In addition, bigger and more effective disc brakes were fitted, a limited-slip differential was standard fitment and the aerodynamics were improved by the adoption of plexiglass cowls over the headlights.

The results were outstanding: the DB4 GT accelerated from 0-60mph in a fraction over six seconds and on to 100mph in just over 14 seconds. At the same time, top speed increased to 153mph (246km/h).

Only 75 DB4 GT cars were produced between 1959 and 1963, and sold in the UK for £4,534. More recently, this iconic British sports car is valued at over a million dollars.

Country of Origin:	UK
Body Design:	Touring
Manufacture Date:	1959-63
Power:	302bhp (183kW) @ 6000rpm
Maximum Torque:	240 lb.ft (325Nm) @ 5000rpm
Top Speed:	153mph (246km/h)
0-60mph (0-97km/h):	6.4 secs
Transmission:	4-speed manual
Engine:	3,670cc straight six
Length:	4318mm (170 in.)
Width:	1676mm (66 in.)
Wheelbase:	2362mm (93 in.)
Kerb Weight:	1269kg (2791 lbs.)
Brakes:	Girling discs
Suspension:	Upper and lower wishbones with telescopic shock absorbers and anti-roll bar (F); Live hypoid axle on trailing arms with transverse Watts linkage, coil springs and lever arm shock absorbers (R)
Auction Sale:	2010 £749,133 (€878,955; $1,155,000)

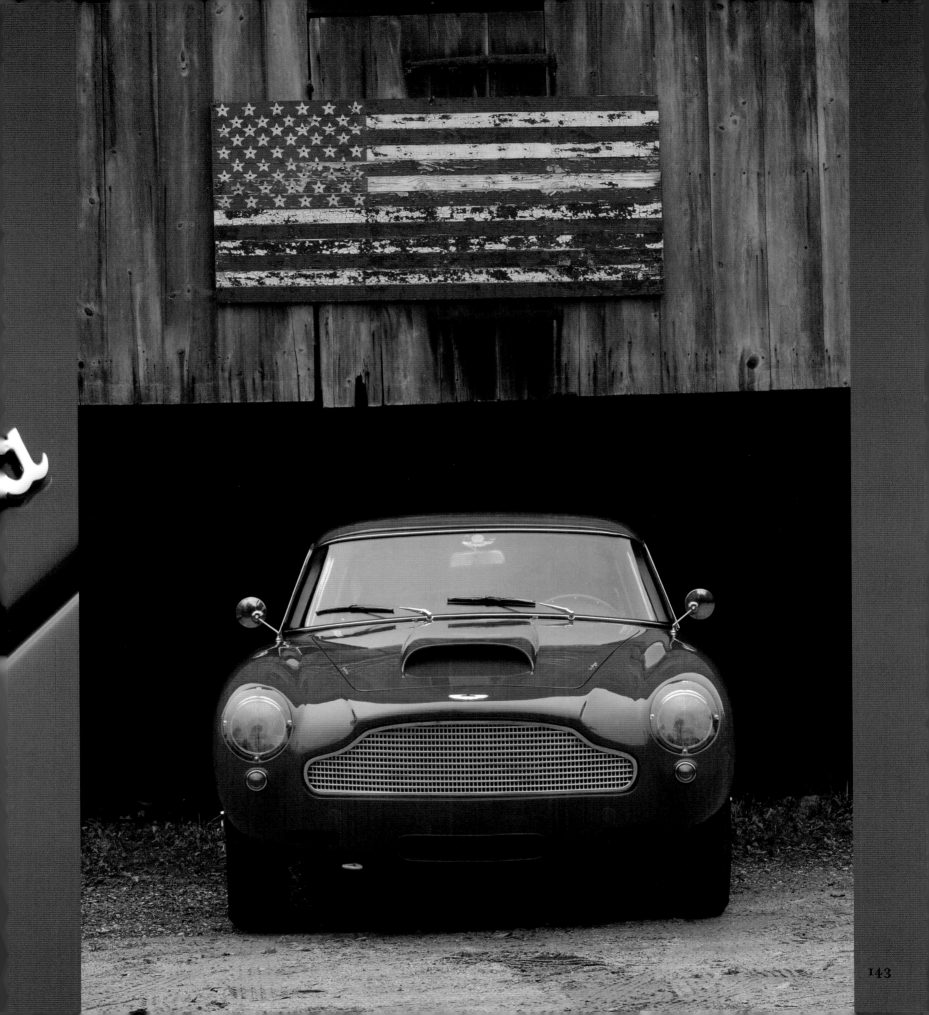

1960 MASERATI TIPO 61 "BIRDCAGE"

The Maserati Tipo 61 — almost always known as the "Birdcage" — was one of the great sports racing cars of the 1960s. It got its name from its highly intricate tubular space frame construction which consisted of some 200 different sections of 10mm and 15mm tubing which when welded created a light but immensely rigid structure. Lightweight aluminium body panels were mounted on the frame and this design resulted in a total weight of just 600kg (1323 lbs.). Match that with the 250bhp (186kW) produced by its twin-cam four-cylinder engine and the Tipo 61 was an instant success on the track, winning first time out at the hands of Stirling Moss in the 1959 Delamare-Deboutteville Cup at that year's Rouen GP meeting.

Sadly that success wouldn't be maintained in Europe because although the Maserati Birdcage proved itself to be extremely fast, it suffered many reliability problems. As a result, although Stirling Moss and Dan Gurney won the 1960 Nürburgring 1000-km race, it failed to win the overall World Sports Car Championship and never won at Le Mans either. In the USA however, the Birdcage had more success in the SCCA Championships of 1960 and 1961 driven by Gus Audrey and Roger Penske.

The original Tipo 60 cars — of which only six were built — had been powered by 2-litre engines producing 195bhp (145kW) but once it had proved its potential a more potent 3-litre engine was fitted. It added a little to the overall weight but its 250bhp output more than compensated. Interestingly, both engines were canted over at a 45-degree angle under the bonnet in order to achieve the smallest possible frontal area and therefore the most efficient aerodynamic performance.

The transmission was a standard Maserati five-speed manual unit mated to a ZF limited slip differential. Suspension was fairly conventional with coil springs and dampers and wishbones at the front, and a De Dion rear axle with transverse leaf spring and telescopic dampers. Girling disc brakes all round provided excellent braking performance, which contributed to the Maserati Birdcage's outstanding lap times.

Despite its mixed success on the track, the car remains one of the all-time greats, in part because of its extreme rarity. Just 16 examples of the Tipo 61 were manufactured, plus one more that was upgraded from the earlier Tipo 60 specification. The cost to private motorsport enthusiasts in 1960 was some £3,900, but the car's value today is counted in the millions.

Country of Origin:	Italy
Body Design:	Giulio Alfieri
Manufacture Date:	1959-1960
Power:	250bhp (186kW) @ 6800rpm
Maximum Torque:	n.a.
Top Speed:	177mph (285km/h)
0-60mph (0-97km/h):	n.a.
Transmission:	5-speed manual
Engine:	2,996cc four-cylinder
Length:	3800mm (149.6 in.)
Width:	1500mm (59.1 in.)
Wheelbase:	2200mm (86.6 in.)
Kerb Weight:	600kg (1320 lbs.)
Brakes:	Discs front and rear
Suspension:	Independent unequal length wishbones and coil-spring dampers (F); De Dion axle with transverse spring and radius rods (R)
Auction Sale:	£1,712,304 (€2,009,040; $2,640,000)

1961 FERRARI 250 GT SWB BERLINETTA SEFAC HOT ROD

Ferrari had launched the 250 GT in 1954 as a high-speed touring car in which gentlemen racers could also compete at the highest levels, should they wish to do so. The Pininfarina-bodied coupé was not just fast, it was also sleekly designed with a beautifully balanced style. Sergio Pininfarina himself described the 250 HT as "the first of our three quantum leaps in design with Ferrari". But it was not just good looking: It also performed wonderfully, clocking up numerous wins in the following years.

For the 1959 season a lightweight body was introduced, designed by Pininfarina but built by Scaglietti and this showed promise at the 24 Hours of Le Mans, coming fourth and sixth. Ferrari then decided that a shorter wheelbase would make the car more competitive and reduced the wheelbase to 94.5 inches (2400mm) to create the 250 GT SWB Berlinetta.

Around 200 of these short-wheelbase racers were built, which, whether driven by amateur or professional drivers, clocked up an impressive number of class wins around the world.

But by 1961 Ferrari was facing increased competition from Jaguar, Aston Martin and Porsche so Enzo Ferrari decided to up the ante once again, reducing the weight and boosting the power of the 250 GT SWB in a limited run of 20 competition cars officially designated Comp/61. At the time, Ferrari had set up a competition department with French industrialist Michel Cavallier called Societa Esercizio Fabbriche Automobili e Corse and very soon, these latest racers became known as the SEFAC Hot Roads as a result of their ultra-low weight, higher power and tuned suspension.

Testa Rossa cylinder heads with bigger valves, high-lift camshafts, a higher compression ratio and a revised exhaust system boosted power to 280bhp at 7,000rpm. This revised engine was mounted in a lighter and stiffer chassis that offered a combination of rugged reliability, superb handling and wonderful balance.

No wonder that the new car dominated in every form of racing during the 1961 season, taking first in class at Le Mans and outright victories in the Targa Florio and RAC Tourist Trophy. It outclassed all its international competitors despite its one major drawback which was its poor aerodynamics. This was something that Ferrari put right in the model that finally surpassed the 250 GT SWB —the seminal Ferrari 250 GTO in 1962.

Meanwhile, the 250 GT SWB Berlinetta SEFAC Hot Rod remains a rare and highly desirable car to collectors, as was proven in late 2010 when a fine example achieved $6,105,000 at auction.

Country of Origin:	Italy
Body Design:	Pininfarina
Manufacture Date:	1961-63
Power:	280bhp (209kW) @ 7000rpm
Maximum Torque:	195 lb.ft (264Nm) @ 5000rpm
Top Speed:	160mph (257km/h)
0-60mph (0-97km/h):	5.0 secs
Transmission:	4-speed manual
Engine:	2,953cc V12
Length:	4430mm (174.4 in.)
Width:	1980mm (78 in.)
Wheelbase:	2400mm (94.5 in.)
Kerb Weight:	1025kg (2255 lbs.)
Brakes:	Discs
Suspension:	Double wishbones, coil springs, telescopic dampers (F); Live axle, semi-elliptic leaf springs, parallel arms, telescopic dampers (R)
Auction Sale:	2010 £3,959,703 (€4,645,905; $6,105,000)

1962 ASTON MARTIN DB4 ZAGATO

Despite being shorter and lighter than the standard Aston Martin DB4, the DB4 GT was still too heavy to compete on even terms on the racetrack with the Ferrari 250 SWB Berlinetta. As a result, an agreement was signed for semi-completed Aston Martin chassis to be shipped to the Zagato works in Milan, Italy for a new lightweight body to be fitted.

There, Ercole Spada created one of the most beautiful bodies that had been seen to date, one that was not only elegant and slippery but which – crucially – was some 45kg (99 lbs.) lighter than the standard GT's. He achieved this by swapping steel components for lighter aluminium wherever possible, removing non-essential items such as bumpers altogether, stripping out the interior and making greater use of Plexiglass instead of glass.

In terms of design, Spada retained much of the basic shape of the standard DB4 GT's Touring body and also retained Aston Martin's traditional grill shape. He also lowered the front of the bonnet so much that bulges had to be introduced on to the top of the bonnet to provide clearance for the valve covers. At the back, the boot had just enough room for the spare wheel and a large fuel tank.

Under the bonnet was an uprated version of the DB4 GT power unit producing 314bhp at 6,000rpm, sufficient to power the Zagato from 0-60mph in 6.1 seconds, and on to a top speed of 153mph (246 km/h).

The DB4 GT Zagato was first unveiled at the 1960 London Motor Show and made an immediate mark, being raced on its first outing by Stirling Moss at the Easter meeting at Goodwood in 1961 when he took third place. Later in the season the Zagato had its first victory at the Silverstone Grand Prix support race. Zagatos also competed at the 24 Hours of Le Mans races in 1961, '62 and '63.

When launched in 1960, a DB4 Zagato cost £5,470 and the company struggled to sell the 25 examples originally planned. In the event, just 19 were built before production ceased in 1963, but the car got a new lease of life in 1991 when four original but unused chassis were sent to Zagato which produced "Works Approved Replicas". A further two "Sanction" cars were built in 2000 using body shells that Zagato had left over. These modern day classics sold for over $1,000,000 each but the originals are still the more desirable to collectors – hence in 2005 a 1961 DB4 GT Zagato was unsold at auction despite a high bid of $2,450,000.

Country of Origin:	UK
Body Design:	Ercole Spada
Manufacture Date:	1960-63
Power:	314bhp (234kW) @ 6000rpm
Maximum Torque:	278 lb.ft (377Nm) @ 5400rpm
Top Speed:	153mph (246km/h)
0-60mph (0-97km/h):	6.1 secs
Transmission:	4-speed manual
Engine:	3,670cc straight six
Length:	4267mm (168 in.)
Width:	1557mm (61.3 in.)
Wheelbase:	2362mm (93 in.)
Kerb Weight:	1225kg (2695 lbs.)
Brakes:	Girling discs
Suspension:	Upper and lower wishbones with telescopic shock absorbers and anti-roll bar (F); Live hypoid axle on trailing arms with transverse Watts linkage, coil springs and lever arm shock absorbers (R)
Estimated Value:	£1.61-1.94 million (€1.89-2.27 million; $2.5-3million)

1962 FERRARI 250 GT CALIFORNIA SPYDER SWB

Ferrari commissioned Pininfarina to design a cabriolet version of the revised 250 GT, which was launched in 1956. Pininfarina's work was first shown at the Geneva Motor Show in 1957 and that car was then extensively used by F1 driver Peter Collins, who had the disc brakes removed and replaced with Dunlop discs – which made this the first Ferrari fitted with discs.

But despite Collins' efforts, the Pininfarina cabriolet had no real pretension to being a competition car. Its steel body was too heavy and its luxurious trim was hardly what was expected of a racing car.

In the USA, importers John von Neumann and Luigi Chinetti managed to persuade Ferrari that there was a market for just that sort of car – a convertible that could be taken serious racing. As a result, Ferrari produced a slimmed down and stripped out derivative of the more powerful 250 GT Tour de France and sales started in the USA in late 1957 of the new 250 GT California Spyder. Though it looked very similar to the Pininfarina cabriolet, the body was actually the work of Scaglietti because Pininfarina was fully stretched producing the cabriolet bodies. All California bodies are very similar, though owners could choose whether to have open or covered headlights.

In truth, even that car was not entirely suited to the racetrack, mainly because of its elongated wheelbase and overall weight. But in 1960 a revised California Spyder was introduced with a more powerful engine, improved braking and suspension and, most importantly of all, a shorter wheelbase that was made possible because Ferrari had created a new and shorter chassis for the 250 GT Berlinetta. With the new chassis reduced from 2600mm wheelbase to 2400mm, not only was the car's handling improved but its overall weight was reduced too.

Power was up from 240bhp to 280bhp, thanks to a revised cylinder head incorporating 12 separate inlet ports, while the clutch was uprated to racing spec, disc brakes were by now standard and the suspension was beefed up with telescopic dampers in place of the older lever dampers.

The result was not just a very quick car, but one of the most beautiful Ferrari's of all time. 57 SWB California Spyders were built between 1960 and 1963 and these have now become one of the most prized of all Ferraris. When the Hollywood actor James Coburn's former 250 GT SWB California Spyder was auctioned in 2008, it went for over €7 million – at the time the highest price ever paid for a car at auction.

Country of Origin:	Italy
Body Design:	Scaglietti
Manufacture Date:	1960-63
Power:	280bhp (208.7kW) @ 7000rpm
Maximum Torque:	203 lb.ft (275Nm) @ 5500rpm
Top Speed:	160mph (257km/h)
0-60mph (0-97km/h):	7.0 secs
Transmission:	4-speed manual with overdrive
Engine:	2,953cc V12
Length:	4200mm (165.4 in.)
Width:	1720mm (67.7 in.)
Wheelbase:	2400mm (94.4 in.)
Kerb Weight:	1065kg (2350 lbs.)
Brakes:	Discs
Suspension:	Double wishbones, coil springs, telescopic dampers (F); Live axle, coil springs, telescopic dampers (R)
Auction Sale:	2008 £6,004,377 (€7,040,000; $9,304,785)

1962 FERRARI 330 TRI/LM TESTA ROSSA

All Ferraris with a competition history are special, but the Ferrari 330 TRI LM is unique — it's the only 4-litre Testa Rossa ever constructed, it was the last of the first series Testa Rossa built, it was the last front-engined sports racing car built by Ferrari and it was the last front-engined car ever to have won at Le Mans.

For the 1962 Le Mans race, the organisers changed the classifications to introduce a new 4-litre class and Enzo Ferrari saw this as an opportunity to develop the Testa Rossa line still further. The 4-litre V12 from the Ferrari Superamerica was shoehorned into an elongated chassis and, with three double Weber carburettors, produced 360bhp initially. But before being taken to Le Mans, Testa Rossa cylinder heads with individual intake ports for each of the 12 cylinders, and six double Weber carburettors was sufficient to boost power output to some 390bhp.

The suspension was similar to earlier Testa Rossas, with double wishbones, coil springs and telescopic dampers front and rear. Bodywork was by Fantuzzi who evolved the familiar GTO shape to incorporate a low nose with twin openings and a high, sharply cut-off Kamm tail to reduce drag and increase top speed. It also had an aerofoil behind the cockpit that improved high-speed stability and also acted as a roll bar. The five-speed gearbox was strengthened and Dunlop disc brakes were further developed to increase stopping power. In fact the one weakness was the clutch, as drivers Phil Hill and Olivier Gendebien — who had won Le Mans the previous year in the 250 TRI — found that to prevent clutch slip they had to change up earlier than they would have liked.

Despite this handicap, they won, taking the chequered flag five laps ahead of the second placed Ferrari 250 GTO. After this famous victory the car was sold to Ferrari's USA importer Luigi Chinetti, whose NART racing team continued to race it until it suffered severe accident damage at the 1963 Le Mans.

After this Chinetti ordered from Fantuzzi both an open Spyder body and a more original coupé body. The Spyder was fitted first, later it was changed for the coupé and later still the car was restored to bring it back to its 1962 Le Mans configuration. In 2002 it sold for $6,500,000, which was then the highest price ever achieved by a Ferrari at auction. The value of this truly unique car has inevitably continued to rise and in 2007 it sold for €6,875,000 (around $9,250,000 at the time) at the RM Leggenda e Passione auction at Maranello, home of Ferrari.

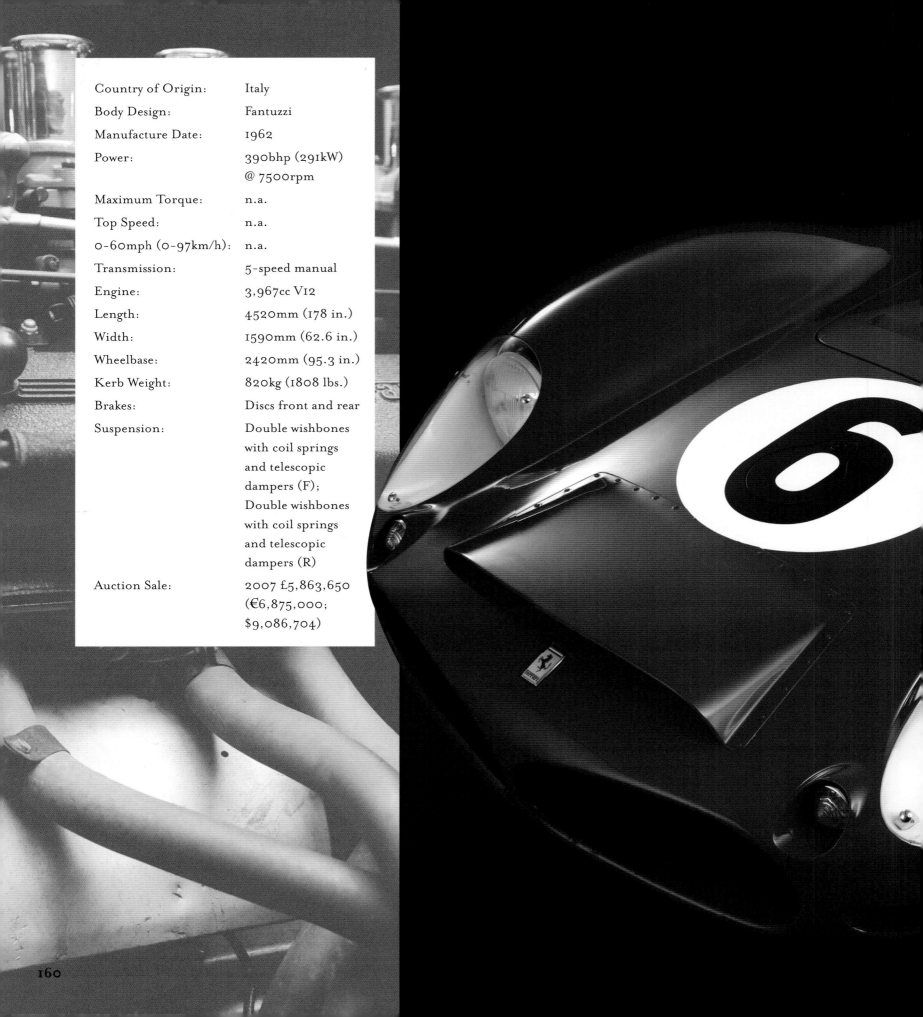

Country of Origin:	Italy
Body Design:	Fantuzzi
Manufacture Date:	1962
Power:	390bhp (291kW) @ 7500rpm
Maximum Torque:	n.a.
Top Speed:	n.a.
0-60mph (0-97km/h):	n.a.
Transmission:	5-speed manual
Engine:	3,967cc V12
Length:	4520mm (178 in.)
Width:	1590mm (62.6 in.)
Wheelbase:	2420mm (95.3 in.)
Kerb Weight:	820kg (1808 lbs.)
Brakes:	Discs front and rear
Suspension:	Double wishbones with coil springs and telescopic dampers (F); Double wishbones with coil springs and telescopic dampers (R)
Auction Sale:	2007 £5,863,650 (€6,875,000; $9,086,704)

1963 FERRARI 250 GTO

The legendary Ferrari GTO was significant not just because it was among the last front-engined cars to win in major international GT and sports car events; it was also important in that it was one of Ferrari's first serious investigations into the art of aerodynamics. With the GTO, he realised that while there were diminishing returns in his efforts to extract extra power from his V12 engines, relatively simple measures such as lowering the nose, minimising cooling drag and adopting a cut-off Kamm tail all helped make the car more aerodynamic, resulting in a higher top speed and better acceleration too.

The FIA introduced what was effectively a new World Championship for Sports Cars in 1962 and to compete — and win — in this championship, Ferrari developed the new 250 GTO. The starting point was the 250GT SWB chassis, though it was considerably revised for the GTO. Under the low front bonnet was the 2,953cc V12 Testa Rossa engine with dry sump and six carburettors that had already been homologated in the 250 GT SWB and Ferrari maintained that the new car was in fact just a development of the older 250 GT and therefore exempt from the requirement to build 100 examples for homologation purposes. Remarkably, the FIA inspectors gave in and so the 250 GT became the 250 GTO (for "omologato").

The car was an instant success, winning first time out at Sebring in 1962, driven by Phil Hill and Olivier Gendebien. The victories kept coming, such that the 250 GTO won three consecutive championships, plus class wins at Le Mans and established itself as one of the most important racing cars of its generation.

It wasn't long before mid-engined racers made the 250 GTO, to all extents and purposes, obsolete as a racing car. Yet the 39 examples that were built remain to this day among the most sought-after, desirable and valuable cars of all time. It's rumoured that at the very peak of the market, one changed hands for $30,000,000 and more recently it's understood that RM Auctions concluded a private treaty sale, reportedly for $18,000,000 to British broadcaster Chris Evans, for chassis number 4675GT, a car that had been owned by a Japanese collector since the mid 1990's.

Some would say that's a small price to pay for one of the most legendary, iconic cars in the world. Because the Ferrari 250 GTO is not just one of the most beautiful cars ever constructed, but one of the most consistently successful in competition too.

Country of Origin:	Italy
Body Design:	Scaglietti
Manufacture Date:	1962–1964
Power:	280bhp (208.8kW) @ 7500rpm
Maximum Torque:	217 lb.ft. (294Nm) @ 5500rpm
Top Speed:	175mph (282km/h)
0-60mph (0-97km/h):	6.1 secs
Transmission:	5-speed manual
Engine:	2,953cc V12
Length:	4400mm (173.2 in.)
Width:	675mm (65.9 in.)
Wheelbase:	2400mm (94.5 in.)
Kerb Weight:	1088kg (2400 lbs.)
Brakes:	Discs front and rear
Suspension:	Double wishbones with coil springs and telescopic dampers (F); Live axle with semi-elliptic leaf springs, parallel arms and telescopic dampers (R)
Private Treaty Sale:	2010 £11,615,400 (€13,618,800; $18,000,000)

1963 SHELBY DAYTONA COUPÉ

Carroll Shelby's Cobra roadster was one of the great successes of sports car racing in the USA during the 1963 season. The car was loosely based on the British AC Ace chassis, into which a Shelby had shoehorned a 221 cubic inch Ford V8 in 1962. After further development, the Ford Fairlane 260 cu. in. engine was made available and the AC Cobra was born, with the first 100 examples being built that year to allow the Cobra to enter the SCCA production class.

The new roadster proved itself both quick and nimble from its very first race and it became even quicker when Ford's 289 cu. in. V8 was adopted. But there was further development in store: While the roadster was winning on America's short tracks, its aerodynamics worked against it the higher speed events that made up the FIA GT World Championship. So Shelby was persuaded to manufacture a bespoke closed cockpit body which in tests proved itself to be around 20mph (32km/h) faster than the roadster.

The first outing of the new Cobra Coupé was at the 1964 Daytona International. It ran strongly until a pit fire put paid to its race but thereafter it became known as the Cobra Daytona Coupé. Soon after, it came fourth in the GT Class at the Sebring 12-Hours race and that was enough for Ford to offer its full backing for an attempt at the prestigious 24 Hours of Le Mans race.

A new chassis – CSX2299 – was sent to Italy for a new body commissioned from the Italian Gransport company to be fitted. At Le Mans that year, driven by Dan Gurney and Bob Bondurant, it won the GT Class and came fourth overall. Importantly for Ford, who had tried to buy Ferrari but been rebuffed and whose GT40 project was not yet ready, the Shelby Daytona trounced the Ferraris at Le Mans. Further successes came at Goodwood, and the following year, at Daytona, Sebring, the Nürburgring and Reims. During 1964 and 65 Gransport completed four new cars to bring the total production run of the Daytona Coupé to six.

Since the Daytona Coupé is such an iconic American racing car and since just six were ever made, values today are inevitably high. Chassis CSX2300 was sold for $4,000,000 in 2000; chassis CSX2601 sold for $7,250,000 in 2009, and were the arguably even more important chassis CSX2299 to come under the hammer it's estimated that it would make as much as $8,000,000.

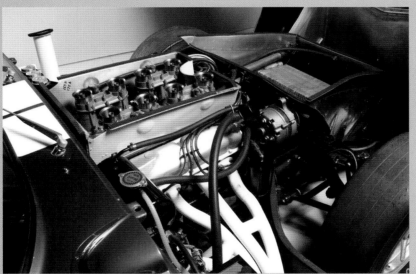

Country of Origin:	UK/USA
Body Design:	Gransport
Manufacture Date:	1964-65
Power:	380bhp (283kW) @ 7000rpm
Maximum Torque:	340 lb.ft (461Nm) @ 4000rpm
Top Speed:	191mph (307km/h)
0-60mph (0-97km/h):	4.0 secs
Transmission:	4-speed manual
Engine:	4,727cc V8
Length:	4150mm (163.4 in.)
Width:	1720mm (67.7 in.)
Wheelbase:	2290mm (90.2 in.)
Kerb Weight:	1043kg (2299 lbs.)
Brakes:	Discs
Suspension:	Lower wishbones, with transverse leaf springs and shock absorbers (F); Lower wishbones, with transverse leaf springs and shock absorbers (R)
Estimated Value:	£5,162,400 (€6,052,800; $8,000,000)

1964 ASTON MARTIN DB5

In Ian Fleming's books, James Bond tended to drive a 1930 gunmetal-coloured Bentley 4½ litre fitted with a Villiers supercharger. In the films, however, the spy with the licence to kill has been seen in a Lotus, a Citroën 2CV, various BMW's and more recently in an Aston Martin V12 Vanquish and an Aston Martin DBS V12.

But perhaps the most famous Bond car of all is another Aston Martin – the DB5 that Sean Connery drove first in Goldfinger and later in Thunderball. Four cars in all were actually used for filming and promotion and one of the film cars was stolen and is believed to have been destroyed. The cars that are left – and most especially the only car left that was actually used in the films – are worth millions now. Even the standard road cars – which cost from £4175 in 1963 – now fetch up to £350,000 at auction.

The Aston Martin DB5 looks very similar to its predecessor, the DB4, and only just over 1,000 examples were made during its two year production cycle from 1963 to 1965.

Its 3,995cc straight six engine produced 282bhp (210kW) at 5,500rpm and 288 lb.ft (380Nm) of torque at 4,500rpm, giving it a top speed of 145mph (233km/h) and 0-60mph (0-97km/h) acceleration in 7.1 seconds. In 1964, a faster Vantage model was introduced with power boosted to 325bhp (242kW) at 5,500rpm.

The elegant bodywork could be specified in either saloon or convertible format, though in addition just 12 ultra-rare Shooting Breaks were made. Although the cars were constructed in the UK, the bodywork was made under licence from Touring in Italy whose "Superleggera" (Super Light) construction method consisted of a lightweight tubular structure over which lightweight aluminium body panels were fitted. The result not only displays a timeless elegance, but the weight reduction also boosted the car's outright performance and aided its handling.

By today's standards, the performance is pretty tame. But what made this DB5 very special was its unique specification that included machine guns, a bullet-proof rear shield, a revolving number plate, tracking device, oil slick sprayer, smoke screen and even an ejector seat.

The guns and ejector seat may not be real, but the James Bond DB5 most certainly is. It's a unique example of what has become an iconic model over the years, and one which is regularly voted one of the most beautiful British luxury sports cars ever made.

Country of Origin:	UK
Body Design:	Aston Martin
Manufacture Date:	1963-1965
Power:	282bhp (210kW) @ 5500rpm
Maximum Torque:	288 lb.ft (390Nm) @ 2350rpm
Top Speed:	145mph (233km/h)
0-60mph (0-97km/h):	7.1 secs
Transmission:	5-speed manual
Engine:	3,995cc straight six
Length:	4572mm (180 in.)
Width: 1	676mm (66 in.)
Wheelbase:	2489mm (98 in.)
Kerb Weight:	1468kg (3229 lbs.)
Brakes:	Girling Twin Servo assisted discs
Suspension:	Independent coil springs, upper and lower wishbones, telescopic shock absorbers (F); Live Hypoid axle on parallel trailing links, Watts linkage, helical coil springs with Armstrong double acting lever arm shock absorbers (R)
Auction Sale:	2010 £2,912,000 (€3,414,256; $4,512,630

1964 FORD GT40 PROTOTYPE

The legendary Ford GT40 owes its very existence to a business deal that went sour. In the early 1960s the American car giant opened negotiations to buy 90% of the shares of the Italian supercar manufacturer Ferrari. A price of some $10,000,000 was more or less agreed but the insurmountable sticking point was Ferrari's future racing activities. The deal as structured would have also given Ford 10% of Ferrari's racing division but Enzo Ferrari was determined that he would retain absolute control over when and where Ferrari would compete.

When the deal fell apart – due to what Ford's CEO Henry Ford II saw as Enzo Ferrari's intransigence – he ordered Ford's Advanced Vehicle Division to get to work immediately to produce a car that would humiliate Ferrari where it would hurt him most – on the racetracks of Le Mans and other long distance GT racing venues.

Sure enough, in April 1964 a new, low-slung, beautifully proportioned and purposeful-looking competitor was unveiled – the GT40. It was based on a Lola GT that had already been under development and it looked the part but was sadly uncompetitive.

For the 1965 season, development was entrusted to Carroll Shelby who worked his magic on the GT40, retaining the monocoque structure but fitting the ultra-reliable Ford 289 cu. in. V8 that had provided such good service in the competition Shelby Cobra. The car finished first time out as Ken Miles and Lloyd Ruby took the chequered flag at the season opener in Daytona at an astonishing average speed of 99.9mph (160.7km/h). Better still for Ford, the top five finishers were two GT40's and three Ford-powered Shelby Daytona Coupes, while the three works Ferraris all failed to finish.

The following year, Ford completed its task of humiliating Ferrari when GT40s came first, second and third at Le Mans. A GT40 won again in 1967 after which the cars ran under Gulf sponsorship and won yet again at Le Mans in both 1968 and 1969.

The GT40 (named because it is a Grand Turismo and just 40 inches in height) has since become a truly iconic model. Around 126 examples are believed to have been built and a number of different engines were offered, starting with a 255 cubic-inch. 289, 302, 351 and 427 cu. in. engines were also fitted at various times.

Every GT40 is special but the prototype that won the car's first ever race at Daytona stands out from them all. Its original 289 engine has since been replaced by a 255 cu. in. Indy powerplant but it remains highly original and highly significant historically.

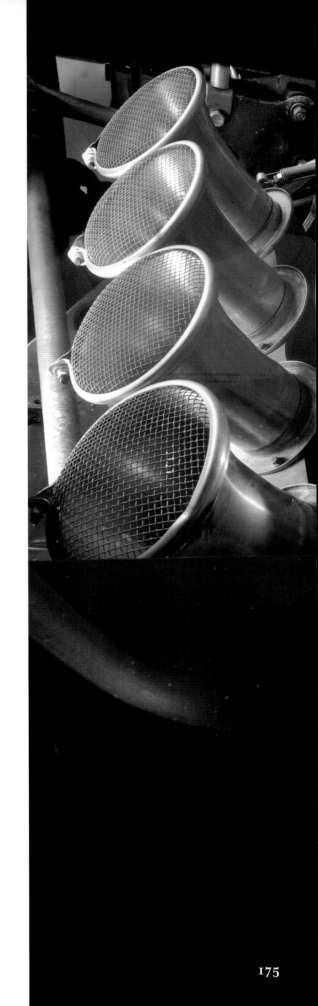

Country of Origin:	USA
Body Design:	Ford
Manufacture Date:	1964–66
Power:	350bhp (268kW) @ 7,200rpm
Maximum Torque:	290 lb.ft (393Nm) @ 5,600rpm
Top Speed:	164mph (264km/h)
0–60mph (0–97km/h):	5.3 secs
Transmission:	5-speed manual
Engine:	255 cu. in (4,184cc) V8
Length:	4028mm (159 in.)
Width:	1778mm (70 in.)
Wheelbase:	2421mm (95 in.)
Kerb Weight:	862kg (1,900 lbs.)
Brakes:	Ventilated discs
Suspension:	Double wishbone with anti-roll bar and coil springs and shock absorbers (F); Double trailing links, transverse top link and lower wishbone with coil springs and shock absorbers (R)
Price at Auction:	2005 £1,614,863 (€1,893,391; $2,502,500)

1964 SHELBY COBRA TEAM CSX 2431

AC Cars, based in Kingston-upon-Thames to the south-west of London, was one of many British independent car manufacturers, but by the early 1960's it was producing no more than a handful of Bristol-engined AC Ace roadsters and AC Aceca coupés. At the time they offered a good turn of performance, with a top speed of 117mph (188km/h) and acceleration from 0-60mph in some 7.4 seconds.

Former American racer Carroll Shelby recognised that the chassis had far more potential and he approached AC with a proposal to fit a large 221 cu. in. Ford V8 engine and transmission to the Ace and sell the car in far greater volumes in the USA. The first two engines were duly shipped to the UK in 1961 and fitted along with a Borg-Warner gearbox which was connected to a British Salisbury rear differential.

Some development work was needed because of the vastly increased power of the Ford V8, but generally the adaptation went very smoothly, so smoothly in fact that when Ford later made available its even bigger 260 cu. in. and even 289 cu. in. V8s, these too were installed with few problems.

The result was a fabulously quick and agile car that not only made an outstanding road car, but which also immediately proved itself on the racetrack. Two cars were entered into the 1963 24 Hours of Le Mans, Shelby's retiring with mechanical problems, while the AC factory car completed the distance and came a creditable seventh after clocking a maximum speed of 161mph (259km/h).

The following years, 1964 and 1965, Shelby's American team driver Ken Miles not only produced impressive race results, but he also worked with Shelby, using chassis CSX 2431 to test and develop the Shelby team race cars including the Daytona Coupé. Among the modifications first introduced on the car was the side-draft Weber carburettor and manifold design that added a further 75bhp to the 289 cu. in. V8's already hefty output.

A proud British citizen, Ken Miles always drove with BRDC (British Racing Drivers' Club) logos prominently displayed on the doors of his car.

Early Shelby Cobras are among the most sought-after sports cars of their era, with a number having changed hands in recent years for between $1,000,000 and $2,000,000. But were this chassis CSX 2431 to be offered for sale, its value would be significantly higher because it's generally held to be the Cobra with the most important racing history. As a result, it's estimated to be worth around $2,500,000.

Country of Origin:	UK/USA
Body Design:	AC Cars
Manufacture Date:	1964–65
Power:	271bhp (199.5kW) @ 5750rpm
Maximum Torque:	312 lb.ft (423Nm) @ 4500rpm
Top Speed:	135mph (217km/h)
0–60mph (0–97km/h):	5.0 secs
Transmission:	4-speed manual
Engine:	4,727cc (289 cu. in.) V8
Length:	3960mm (156 in.)
Width:	1720mm (67.7 in.)
Wheelbase:	2290mm (90.2 in.)
Kerb Weight:	1045kg (2300 lbs.)
Brakes:	Discs
Suspension:	Lower wishbones, with transverse leaf springs and shock absorbers (F); Lower wishbones, with transverse leaf springs and shock absorbers (R)
Estimated Value:	£1,613,250 (€1,891,500; $2,500,000)

1966 FERRARI 250 LM

Enzo Ferrari had a reputation for stretching the rules if it might give his cars a competitive advantage, but his efforts to pull the wool over the authorities' eyes with the 250 LM model in the early 1960's was a step too far.

At the time, to race in the FIA GT Championship, a minimum of 100 production examples had to be built. Enzo Ferrari got round this with the 250 GTO in 1962 which was homologated even though only 39 were built, but Ferrari successfully argued that it was only a rebodied version of the 250 GT SWB.

He then went ahead to build the 250 LM, a fabulous car allegedly destined for both road and track, and one which would have been Ferrari's first ever mid-engined road car. By 1964, with just a handful built, Ferrari claimed it should be homologated on the grounds it was a further development of the 250 GTO. This time, however, the authorities baulked, understandably insisting that moving the engine from the front to the midships constituted far more than an evolution.

The result was that the 250 LM had to be entered in the prototype class rather than the GT class but it proved its worth, albeit with a little bit of luck along the way. On paper the 250 LM was outclassed by the new Ford GT40 but in the 1965 Le Mans race, it was a Ferrari 250 LM entered by Luigi Chinetti's NART team that took the chequered flag, driven by Jochen Rindt and Masten Gregory. That year, all the GT40's retired, as did the work's Ferraris, but that didn't make the 250 LM's victory any less momentous.

The 250 LM was first revealed at the 1963 Paris Motor Show, and that car had a 2,933cc V12 mounted behind the cockpit. All the later cars had a 3,286cc V12 and should strictly have been called 275 LM according to Ferrari's naming system but perhaps in order to maintain the fiction that the car was a development of the 250 GTO, the original 250 LM name was retained.

Just 32 250 LM's were built, of which one was trimmed by Pininfarina with a red leather interior and electric windows for road use. All the rest were racers, entered by the likes of NART in the USA, Maranello Concessionaires in the UK, Scuderia Filipinetti in Switzerland and Ecurie Francorchamps in Belgium.

Inevitably, all Ferraris with a proven racing history are highly valued and rarely come up for sale. The most recent 250 LM sale was for $5,700,000.

Country of Origin:	Italy
Body Design:	Pininfarina
Manufacture Date:	1963-1966
Power:	320bhp (239kW) @ 8000rpm
Maximum Torque:	294Nm (217 lb.ft.) @ 5500rpm
Top Speed:	160mph (257km/h)
0-60mph (0-97km/h):	6.1 secs
Transmission:	5-speed manual
Engine:	3,286cc V12
Length:	4090mm (161 in.)
Width:	1700mm (66.9 in.)
Wheelbase:	2400mm (94.5 in.)
Kerb Weight:	861kg (1900 lbs.)
Brakes:	Discs front and rear
Suspension:	Double wishbones with coil springs and telescopic dampers (F); Double wishbones with coil springs and telescopic dampers (R)
Private Sale:	2005 £3,678,210 (€4,312,620; $5,700,000)

1967 FERRARI NART SPYDER

During the 1950s and 1960s one of the most important men in the development of the Ferrari brand was Luigi Chinetti, Ferrari's East Coast importer. It was he who persuaded Ferrari to develop the 250 GT California in 1957, primarily for the US market, and it was again Chinetti who pressed for a convertible version of the Ferrari 275 GTB/4 in 1966.

At first Enzo Ferrari declined because the company had just launched the luxurious 330 GTS Spyder. But Chinetti – who had won Le Mans for Ferrari in 1949 and whose feel for the wishes of US customers was undoubtedly accurate – persisted in pressing for a stripped out, hardcore performance Spyder.

Eventually, Ferrari relented and commissioned Scaglietti to create an aluminium roadster body in 1967 which Chinetti quickly fitted with a roll-bar and entered into the Sebring 24-Hours. It came second in class, despite a complete lack of race preparation and was dubbed the Ferrari NART Spyder (for North American Racing Team, Chinetti's competition outfit).

Under the bonnet was a 3.3-litre V12 with four camshafts – which explains the name GTB/4 – and six Weber carburettors. Its output was 300bhp in standard form and 330bhp in competition tune. The independent suspension was carried over from the Pininfarina designed 275 GTB/4, as was the five-speed transaxle which helped ensure the optimum weight distribution.

Perhaps over-optimistically, Chinetti ordered 25 NART Spyders from the factory though in fact only ten were delivered and, amazingly, Chinetti had to sell most of them at a discount. Of the ten sold, just two had the original aluminium body, which was then dropped in favour of a slightly heavier, but less expensive steel body.

One of the 275/4 NART Spyder's most famous customers was movie actor Steve McQueen who drove the actual Sebring race car in the film "The Thomas Crown Affair". It was a clever piece of product placement by Chinetti, not least because McQueen promptly placed an order. To suit the requirements of Hollywood, however, Chinetti had to re-spray the car a burgundy colour as it was felt this would film better than the original pale yellow "Giallo Solare" paint finish.

The car was later sold to Norman Silver, who returned the car to its original colour and kept it in his collection until his death in 1985. Another NART Spyder was sold for $2,000,000 in 1998 but the original chassis 09437 car, because of its aluminium body and its history, is inevitably worth more. Sure enough, when offered at auction in 2005 the hammer fell at $3,960,000.

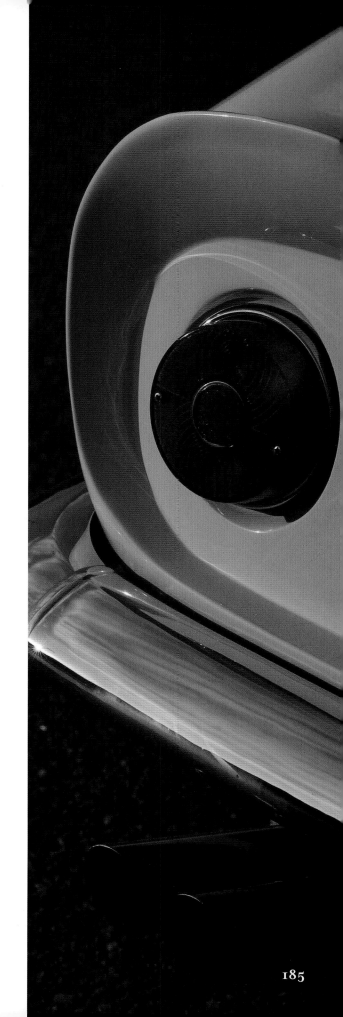

Country of Origin:	Italy
Body Design:	Scaglietti
Manufacture Date:	1967-1968
Power:	300bhp (223.7kW) @ 8000rpm
Maximum Torque:	294.2Nm (217 lb.ft.)
Top Speed:	155mph (250km/h)
0-60mph (0-97km/h):	6.7 secs.
Transmission:	5-speed manual
Engine:	3,286cc V12
Length:	4409mm (173.6 in.)
Width:	1725mm (67.9 in.)
Wheelbase:	2400mm (94.5 in.)
Kerb Weight:	1114kg (2456 lbs.)
Brakes:	Discs front and rear
Suspension:	Double wishbones with coaxial coil springs and telescopic dampers (F); Double wishbones with coaxial coil springs and telescopic dampers (R)
Action Sale:	2005 £2,555,388 (€2,996,136; $3,960,000)

1996 McLaren F1

Gordon Murray, the man behind the development of the McLaren F1, had very firm ideas of what he wanted to achieve. It would be the world's fastest and purest performance car, built without regard to cost. It would be powered by a naturally-aspirated engine, because the response of a turbocharged unit would not be sufficiently immediate. Its weight would be kept to an absolute minimum. And there would be as few electronic driver aids as possible – so no traction control and not even an ABS braking system.

The monocoque chassis was constructed from carbon fibre – the world's first production car to employ this expensive technology. Titanium, magnesium, Kevlar and even gold (to reflect the heat of the engine) were employed as part of the specification of the ultimate road car.

Murray had originally wanted to use a Honda engine, derived from the current McLaren-Honda F1 car but when this proved impossible he turned to BMW who created for the McLaren F1 a new V12 producing 626bhp (468kW) and 480 lb.ft (651Nm) of torque. Combined with the car's light weight, this was enough to offer 0-60mph acceleration in 3.2 seconds and a top speed of 231mph (372km/h) – making it comfortably the world's fastest production car, an honour it held for many years.

The car would also be as compact as possible and to achieve this Murray opted for an unusual seating arrangement, with the driver sitting centrally and a further two passenger seats set a little further back in the cockpit. When the McLaren F1 was launched, it was claimed that this seating arrangement was unique, though in fact it had been proposed as long ago as 1947 on a Lancia prototype.

As an integral part of Murray's quest for purity in both engineering and design, the Peter Stevens bodywork employed no overt spoilers though there was an unobtrusive rear spoiler that adjusted under heavy braking to balance the centre of gravity. Overall, the body design, which incorporates a rear diffuser to create a degree of ground effect to increase downforce at high speeds, achieved a drag co-efficient of 0.32.

McLaren originally intended to sell 300 F1 cars but in the event just 106 were manufactured, of which 64 were standard road cars with the remainder prototypes, race cars and a series of five higher specification F1 LM models.

At launch the cost price of the McLaren F1 was $970,000 but the supercars come onto the market so rarely that in 2008 a pristine example was sold for £2,530,000, almost $4 million.

Country of Origin:	UK
Body Design:	Peter Stevens
Manufacture Date:	1993-1998
Power:	627bhp (468kW) @ 7400rpm
Maximum Torque:	479 lb.ft (649Nm) @ 5600rpm
Top Speed:	231mph (372km/h)
0-60mph (0-97km/h):	3.2 secs
Transmission:	6-speed manual
Engine:	6,064cc V12
Length:	4288mm (168.9 in.)
Width:	1820mm (71.7 in.)
Wheelbase:	2718mm (107 in.)
Kerb Weight:	1138kg (2500 lbs.)
Brakes:	Ventilated discs
Suspension:	Double wishbones with light alloy dampers and coaxial coil springs (F); Double wishbones with light alloy dampers and coaxial coil springs (R)
Auction Sale:	2008 £2,530,000 (€2,966,369; $3,920,657)

PICTURE CREDITS

Front cover and page 1 – 1960 Maserati Tipo 61 "Birdcage"

Pages 2, 4 – 1936 Mercedes-Benz 540K Cabriolet A

Page 192 – 1939 Mercedes-Benz W154

Back cover – 1966 Ferrari 275 GTB4

All images copyright Simon Clay except for those listed.

www.simonclay.com

Images on the following pages copyright Tom Wood 70, 71, 72, 73, 74, 75 ,76, 77 136, 137, 138, 139, 151, 152, 153, 54, 155, 156, 157, 182, 183, 184, 188, 189, 190, 191

With special thanks to Mark Donaldson for his advice and current pricing estimates.